MEDITATIONS
OF A BROOMSTICK

THIS ?

OR THIS ?

The author observing Ministers discussing Public Expenditure

Meditations
of a Broomstick

LORD ROTHSCHILD

COLLINS
St James's Place, London
1977

William Collins Sons & Co. Ltd
London · Glasgow · Sydney · Auckland
Toronto · Johannesburg

First published 1977
© Lord Rothschild 1977
ISBN 0 00 216512 0
Set in Monotype Baskerville
Made and Printed in Great Britain by
William Collins Sons & Co. Ltd, Glasgow

TO TESS

CONTENTS

ILLUSTRATIONS

'There is nothing more difficult to take in hand, more perilous to conduct, or more uncertain in its success than the introduction of a new order of things, because the innovator has for enemies all those who have done well under the old conditions and lukewarm defenders in those who may do well under the new.'

MACHIAVELLI, *The Prince*

THE BEGINNING

The names of all the boys mentioned in this chapter are fictitious except those of Openshaw, Cremer, Goldschmidt and Pleydell-Bouverie. It cannot be guaranteed that people with these fictitious names do not exist, but if they do, their existence is coincidental.

*

MOST people associate the name Rothschild with banking, in spite of the 1976 London Telephone Directory containing Rothschilds who are Dental Surgeons, Accountants, Physicians, 'Furn Fabrics, Linen', and one who just calls himself Trading Co. There are one hundred and thirty-eight different varieties in the Manhattan Telephone Directory. Though my father went each day to what is always known as 'Rothschilds', in the City of London, he somehow found time to be a scientist as well – quite impossible today – with the result that my sisters and I grew up in an atmosphere of undiluted natural history. My earliest recollection, when I was about four years old, was of being sent into the garden by my father to try to catch a very rare butterfly, a gynandromorph Orange Tip: one which is half male and half female, with its orange tip, therefore, on only one wing. I remember being punished a few years later for going into the long grass without wearing my galoshes (rubbers) to catch another very rare butterfly, an albino Meadow Brown. The sentence was terribly severe: I had to give the white Meadow Brown to my eldest sister. She gave it back to me, beautifully mounted, as a twenty-first birthday present. I have it still, some forty-five years later. It seems a little faded, but of course I now don't know if it is or not.

Rare varieties of common butterflies occupied a special place in our lives, alongside more mundane entomological activities: for example, keeping dug-up bumble bee nests, covered by inverted flower pots, on our bedroom windowsills. That most dedicated of collectors, my uncle the late Lord Rothschild, was, certainly, not immune to the thrill of the chase; and I think I can remember all twenty stone of him lumbering with his butterfly net after the silver variety of the Small Copper. It got away.

My parents, though Liberal in politics, seemed to me severe. Looking back, I do not remember much of what one might expect in a Rothschild house from reading recently published accounts of my family. We were simultaneously spoilt and regimented; and we had little human contact with our parents. In retrospect they were like policemen on traffic duty – stop, go, filter: but they could also endorse one's licence, and did. I remember having spinach for tea because I would not eat it for lunch. I also remember my sister Miriam and myself being coached by a cricket professional who told us wistfully that when he bowled to the great Ranjitsinjhi in the nets at Cambridge there was a gold watch on each stump; he never got one.

Our house seemed full of governesses and tutors. Miss Joyce taught me Latin grammar so mercilessly and efficiently that when, aged eight, I was sent to my preparatory school, Stanmore Park, I was put straight into the top form, only to be demoted after a week to a level more suitable to my age and relative ignorance of everything except Latin grammar. Stanmore Park, I am convinced, was a hell hole. Vernon Royle, the headmaster, was known as 'the Reverend' although not in Holy Orders. He was a famous cricketer. We were told that while he was dozing at cover point one day, a black object hurtled towards him and he caught it. His catch turned out to be a swallow. Under his captaincy the Stanmore Park masters beat the South Africans on tour and one of them, W. N. Roe, who published some quite well-known logarithm tables, made more than four hundred runs in one innings of a first-class match. R. F. Reynolds was a superb shot with a piece of chalk when a boy in his form annoyed him. Nose, cheek, forehead were his three preferred targets, in that order; he never hit a boy in the eye. His classroom was on the second floor and he dangled a boy called Openshaw outside the window, by his hair. Openshaw was not too popular so we were amused. Another master, D. W. Carr, who was said to have invented the googlie before Bosanquet, got drunk one evening and tried to remove the appendix of a boy called Cremer with a penknife. Cremer, who had other difficulties at Stanmore Park, became a good poet later. I was upset when the classics master, J. M. Quinton, who was nice to me, committed suicide in the lavatory of a train; upset by two boys called Schilizzi who were very good at games and bullied many of the small boys; and also upset by one master who used to humiliate me in front of the other boys. There were, of course, some memorable moments of the pleasanter kind at Stanmore Park. I played 'In the Hall of the Mountain King' (Greig's Peer Gynt Suite) alone on the piano on parents' day, which was said to be a great honour; and the school was given a half holiday when I won a scholarship to Harrow school.

I became painfully aware of being a Jew when a boy called Michel kicked my shins shortly after I arrived at Stanmore Park and called me a dirty little Jew. My father and mother were, I suppose, atheists or agnostics. At any rate there was no religious indoctrination at home, though we had to say our prayers, kneeling at our mother's bed, each morning and evening. As far as I can remember, these prayers consisted of asking God to bless all and sundry, including *kind* friends. They ended with a request to make me a good little boy amen. At the time I did not feel there was any detectable response to these injunctions, intoned twice daily under the supervision of my mother or, in her absence, of one or other of the army of nurses and governesses who tried to control us.

Eleven boys were fired from my house at Harrow school in my first term. I did not know why at the time, there having been no indoctrination on such matters either at home or at Stanmore. This lacuna in my education was, however, soon filled: just a fact or a way of life according to inclination or particular circumstances. Being intellectually precocious, no doubt unpleasantly so, I was frequently punished. This usually took the form of a beating – often by the Schilizzis who also went from Stanmore to Harrow – for being cheeky or for 'lip' as it was then called at Harrow. I was frightened of the beatings because they were so painful. A boy called Stilwell knew this and threatened to report me for lip to the head of the house unless I agreed to have a homosexual relationship with him. I was sufficiently unnerved by this blackmail to take the unpardonable step of reporting Stilwell to my house-master, C. G. Pope. Stilwell got into terrible trouble or so it seemed at the time. Until then Mr Pope had disliked me; but after my astonishing behaviour I became one of his favourites and was quite often let off the hateful early morning school. He helped me with a thank-you letter to my Austrian cousin Alphonse – in Greek because my German was not good enough. (Alphonse, who had one of the best stamp collections in the world outside the British Royal family, read only a Latin-Greek dictionary when travelling by train.)

One of the many hideous aspects of life at Harrow school (which is, no doubt, much more civilized now) concerned 'Privileges'. It was a three-year privilege to wear bedroom slippers. The icy stone steps in our house therefore produced very painful chilblains: according to matron, it was through lack of calcium. It was a three-year privilege to whistle (as if one wanted to), to have a hot bath, or to close the lavatory door. A boy called Usborne did not go to the lavatory for a whole term as a result. We were much mystified by this feat of endurance but I suspected he secretly relieved himself at the Music School which, because of its cellular construction, was also the headquarters for homosexual activities. A boy called Whidborne minor, whom I thought particularly beautiful, behaved very badly to an older boy, Hewlett, in the Music School. Whidborne told Hewlett that he could do whatever he liked to him. Hewlett complied with alacrity and imagination, upon which Whidborne screamed and shouted, asserting that he had been indecently assaulted. Hewlett left Harrow on the 4 p.m. train to London the next day. Beautiful as he was Whidborne minor was treated with some reserve and caution from then onwards.

Boredom with the Punic Wars (or the way we were taught about them), and the imbecile behaviour evoked by this boredom, made Mr Pope append a curt note to one of my end of term reports: 'Must do better if he wishes to stay'. The day after this thunderbolt arrived at home I detected some change, which I could not immediately identify, in my mother's study. She quickly solved the puzzle. 'You will see', she said, 'that there are now two desks. The one on the left is my usual one, that on the right is for you. There is a copy of your Roman History textbook and writing paper on yours. Each morning during the holidays you will read about the Punic Wars and write essays which I shall set and correct. If the marks for any particular essay are not high enough, the question will be reset for the next morning.' How did she know about the Punic Wars? When did she mug

them up? In the evenings, instead of playing double dummy
bridge, which she often did? I could not find out, but the results
the next term were electrifying. My essays on Hamilcar Barca and
Massinissa were specially singled out for praise. 'A much better
effort and performance this term', and, after that, Mr Pope
became even more friendly. The amazing thing to me now, more
than fifty years and a number of children later, was my blind
obedience to my mother. 'No way', 'Get lost', 'You must be
joking', or even 'Get stuffed' were not at that time part of the
vocabulary of a boy aged fifteen enjoying a normal, happy
relationship with his parents.

Religious instruction of Jewish boys at Harrow was a continual
source of discussion and dissension. The parents of some Jewish
boys, like my own, were indifferent; others felt that their children
should know something about Judaism. The headmaster, on the
other hand, said that Chapel was not an exercise in proselytization,
but more in the nature of a general address: no more divisive
than a discourse on Britain's coal industry. To begin with,
therefore, non-Christian boys went to Chapel and to Chapel only.
But in the middle of one service, a Persian boy produced a gong
from underneath his tails, hit it three times, then lay down on the
floor of the Chapel with his head facing east. After this episode
the headmaster felt that although attendance at Chapel was
still desirable for infidels, they should also have the benefit of
some other system of instruction more appropriate to their own
religions. Accordingly, each Saturday the Jewish boys were
herded into a classroom known as the Tin Tabernacle, where a
distinguished Shakespearean scholar, Sir Israel Gollancz, attempted to teach them the principles of Judaism. This turned out
to be quite boring and after two Saturdays one very clever Jewish
boy, Tony Goldschmidt (killed in World War II) put a question
to Sir Israel: 'What does the word "Ducdame" mean in *As You
Like It*?' Sir Israel, who seemed as bored by religious indoctrination as we were, reacted with alacrity, erudition and enthusiasm.
So all the Jewish boys got top marks in their papers on *As You
Like It*. Sir Israel was plied with further questions about Shakespeare's plays and sonnets, to his evident enjoyment, but some of
the boys reported to their parents that all religious teaching had
ceased and that the Tin Tabernacle had become a second wooden

O. As a result, Sir Israel left and was replaced by a mediocrity whose name I have forgotten.

Towards the end of my time at Harrow I became good, better, or difficult to ignore at cricket: an automatic passport to popularity which until then had eluded me. I was even allowed to stop re-reading the first chapter of our biology textbook and to progress from *Amoeba* to a higher organism. I had not been permitted to press on before because my friend Pleydell-Bouverie experienced difficulty with or distaste for *Amoeba*; and it was not thought right for one of the two boys studying biology in the top form to get too far ahead of the other. Clearly such a state of affairs would have meant more work for the biology master, D. M. Reid, who, like his pupil, published a classification of the animal kingdom. But being in the cricket eleven and a member of the Harrovian analogue of Pop, called Phil, changed all that. I was given the privilege of abandoning Pleydell-Bouverie to his *Amoeba* and passing on to *Paramoecium*. About that time a nice old boy with a twinkling eye and a frock coat came to Harrow and gave me a *viva* for a scholarship to Cambridge, which I won. He was called Harold Hartley and later became a great friend of mine. I much admired him.

When I arrived home for the vacation after my first term at Cambridge my mother asked me if I had made any new friends (apart from the Harrovians who went to Cambridge at the same time). I had to say I had not, something of which I was very ashamed. She asked the same question each vacation. After a year or so of shame, I was able to announce, and from time to time produce, Garrett Moore (now Lord Drogheda), Dick Sheepshanks (killed in the Spanish Civil War), Sammy Hood, Gerald Cuthbert (killed in World War II), Anthony Blunt and a clever, dissolute young man called Guy Burgess with whom my mother got on very well. Perhaps he was a Soviet agent even then. As a matter of fact, I thought Burgess might have fascist or pro-Nazi inclinations because of his friendship with a good-looking, fair-haired undergraduate of Trinity College called Micky Burn, who was inordinately interested in the Hitler Youth. I now suspect that the friendship between Burgess and Burn was not political.

Having been brought up with butterflies, birds, bees and insects instead of with human beings, I inevitably had a scientific albeit anti-entomological bent (in spite of being made to do classics until the age of sixteen, something for which I am now very grateful). So it came as rather a shock at the age of twenty-one to learn that I was expected at least to try the life of a banker in the City of London. This I did, but the moment was unfortunate. In 1931 there was a world recession; the City seemed moribund, boring, rather painful. I did not like banking which consists essentially of facilitating the movement of money from Point A, where it is, to Point B where it is needed; nor did I like it any more, forty-five years later when, as a temporary expedient, I tried to run Rothschilds for fifteen months. After my first six months in the City I returned to Cambridge University to be a scientist. Except for the war years I lived there until I was forty-eight in a relaxed and, perhaps, somewhat unworldly atmosphere.

The conventional academic progress of a Cambridge undergraduate was, fortunately in the event, disturbed irreparably by a chance remark made to me by the Professor of Zoology at the beginning of my first term. He said to me after one of his lectures: 'I imagine that what you have heard must seem very elementary to you. But you needn't take notes – just put your hands in your pockets'. I was not slow to act on this advice and to go a good deal further than Professor Stanley Gardiner intended. Not to put too fine a point on it, I became completely idle in my scientific studies, apart from those small sections which interested me. As time went on, it became clear that I was unlikely to do as well in Part I of the Natural Sciences Tripos examinations as early promise indicated and my family's wishes required. I therefore persuaded the Professor and his Reader, Dr (later Sir James) Gray, to allow me to attend the Part II Tripos lectures and practicals and to start researching for a doctorate on a project suggested by Dr Gray. Amazing as it may seem, the Statutes of Cambridge University at that time allowed one to research for a Ph.D. without a degree. Life became very pleasant until, at short notice, the Statutes were changed and I had to get a Degree in a hurry. Having done so little work on the syllabus for the Natural Sciences Tripos, I decided to take an Ordinary or Pass Degree in Physiology (which was easy for me), French (which was hardly more difficult because of all those governesses) and English. The last of these was not at all easy because we had not been encouraged to read as children. *Alice in Wonderland*, for example, was forbidden, presumably because my mother had read Freud. Nor did I stir myself to read even such approved works as those of Tennyson and, particularly, of James Fenimore Cooper. To get through the syllabus for my Ordinary Degree in a single year, I was fortunate in having the help of George Rylands, the authority on Shakespeare and Shakespearean productions. His tutorials took place in the country between Cambridge and Newmarket, accompanied by strawberries and cream; in Monte Carlo where, for the first and last time, I played roulette, to modest advantage; and in more humdrum places of learning. Not only did he teach me to appreciate the English language: he also activated the Rothschild collecting gene. I started acquiring English eighteenth-century first editions, particularly those of Jonathan Swift (hence the title of this book[1]), whose scintillating prose, irony and sense of ridicule much appealed to me. The collection, together with some Swift manuscripts, is now in Trinity College Library.

It would be wrong not to mention that I was greatly helped in my French by Professor Jean Seznec and by the then Dean of Trinity College, Cambridge, Dr H. F. Stewart, an authority on Pascal. Mr (now Sir Anthony) Blunt also assisted me with my French from time to time. As a result of this good fortune, I got an unusual distinction in my contemptible Ordinary Degree – a recorded treble first.

Apart from the pleasures of the hunt and the kill, collecting old books brought me some unexpected and rewarding experiences. I was fortunate enough to acquire the original manuscript of one of Swift's most famous satirical pamphlets, his *Directions to Servants*. I thought this would interest G. M. Trevelyan, then Master of Trinity. I therefore invited him to come and see it. Such was his emotion as he turned the pages that his hands shook violently. I was terrified that he might tear at least one of the fragile leaves clean in half. Fortunately the manuscript emerged intact.

Book-collecting also contributed to my friendship with Maynard Keynes, whose many gifts included treating the young as if they were his contemporaries. He was an avid book-collector. On

[1] Superior figs refer to References on pages 182-183

18

Monday mornings the second-hand book catalogues of Gregory used to arrive at Cambridge from Bath. If there was a volume which specially interested him, usually a seventeenth-century work, he would get out his car and tear off to Bath. More often than not, he told me, his brother Geoffrey had arrived before him: 'As I was going up the steps of Gregory's, he would be coming down – with the book I wanted in his hand.'

When I used to visit him, unannounced, in his room at King's College, I never caught him working. He was always in an arm-chair with his feet up reading an edition of Locke, Hume or some other English philosopher or economist. When did he do his day's work? I never found out. The rumour was that he finished it in bed early in the morning. One day I asked him a question about the British economy and his answer turned out in due course to be wrong. 'Why,' I asked Maynard, 'did you tell me ten days ago that we would not go off the gold standard when in fact we now have?' His answer was characteristic and an example to all, whether savants, politicians, civil servants or ordinary folk. 'Victor,' he said, 'I made a mistake.' He went on to say 'You know, I am the economy's dentist. When it seems in good shape, nobody wants to talk to me or even to see me for a check. It is only when the symptoms of a cavity appear that they call for me. The sad thing is that I believe I could often have prevented the cavity developing.'

The third event in my book-collecting career was less agreeable though equally instructive. I bought a first edition of *Tom Jones*, uncut in boards as the experts say, from an American bookseller, Gabriel Wells. During World War II, a friend of mine, John Hayward, was staying in my house and studying my collection of eighteenth-century first editions. He discovered that the *Tom Jones* was a fake or, more precisely, a made-up copy, that is a complete copy made from a number of incomplete ones, some of which were not first editions. My friends in the book-collecting world urged me to insist on Gabriel Wells's taking the book back and reimbursing me, which he refused to do. They then advised me to sue him, which I did. I was represented in the case by someone who was thought to be very promising, called Gerald Gardiner; and we had an expert witness on *caveat emptor*, another coming young man called Kenneth Diplock. *Caveat emptor* was then, at any rate, a difficult principle. If you bought a vat of glue, there was nothing to stop you from testing before the purchase whether the glue stuck or not. But if you bought a stallion at a horse show in Dublin, it would be difficult to carry out the necessary tests before purchase. Mr Diplock explained these difficulties with formidable panache. In our case we maintained that it would have been insulting to test whether the wares of so distinguished a bookseller as Gabriel Wells were genuine or not. The case was settled out of Court, on terms which were very satisfactory from my point of view.[2]

Mr Gardiner had an unerring gift of anticipating that certain questions put to me by Mr Holroyd Pearce, Mr Wells's Counsel, might fluster me: invariably, by means of a polite interjection, he steered the cross-examination into calmer waters. Many years later I asked the Lord Chancellor, as Mr Gardiner became, if he remembered the case. He looked, I thought, rather blank. Mr Diplock, on the other hand, when a Lord of Appeal, did remember his appearance as an expert witness. I have not knowingly met Lord Pearce (as he now is) since.

I do not look back on the research I did for my Prize Fellowship of Trinity College or my Ph.D. with pleasure. Much of what I wrote was wrong and wild, whereas the analogous efforts of a friend of mine, Alan Hodgkin, mentioned elsewhere in this book, are virtually as good today as they were when written.[*]

In those days a Prize Fellowship at Trinity College, Cambridge required the candidate to write a dissertation; he also had to take a three-hour examination euphemistically described as 'general knowledge'. The rumour was that you could bring any books you liked into the examination room and go out as often as you wished. It was customary to include in the paper one question which each candidate would certainly be able to answer. For me it was something like 'The Biophysics of the Trout Egg'; for Anthony Blunt it was 'Picasso', and so on. It was also rumoured that each year the Professor of Philosophy, C. D. Broad, set the same question: 'There is as much difference between science and religion as there is between a whale and an elephant. Discuss.' (I suspect Broad had forgotten that elephants

---

[*] *Note for the physiologist.* Saltatory conduction in myelinated nerves had not been discovered at that time.

and whales are both mammals; but one could, I suppose, make comparable remarks about science and religion. Perhaps that is why the question was set.) Nobody knew who, if anyone, corrected or even read the papers; but in due course, if one was successful, a most terrifying event occurred: the Fellowship Admission Dinner, at which in my time the Master, Sir J. J. Thomson (discoverer of the electron), made a speech about the new Fellows, memorable for its tactlessness. Of Anthony Blunt he observed that it was the first occasion on which the College had given a Fellowship to someone who specialized in the history of art; he was confident that it would not occur again. In my case, after a few disparaging remarks about those who 'pricked frogs' eggs' (a biophysical activity in which I was engaged at the time), he went on to congratulate the College on making no distinction between the 'exceedingly rich', pointing at me, and the 'very very poor', pointing at the other successful candidate. That was not my only penance. Next day, walking through the Great Court of Trinity College, I met the Master who greeted me by saying 'What relation are you to the Rothschild to whom we gave a Fellowship last night?'.

J.J., as everyone called the Master, was much loved. On his eightieth birthday, the Fellows of Trinity presented him with an address which read as follows:

TO
SIR JOSEPH JOHN THOMSON, O.M.

THE ANCIENTS WHO FIRST FABLED THAT THE WORLD WAS MADE OF ATOMS taught that these wayward bodies move, for no discoverable reason, in any and every direction. You, Master, to whom the habits of the atom are as a book unsealed, must have remarked how nearly they resemble the behaviour of the members of our society. When we are called upon to determine whether the fountain shall be bordered with flowers or the chapel beleaguered with iron spikes, we meet only to rebound; and the predictable outcome of collision is that we shall be found inextricably revolving in a vortex.

There are, however, some few occasions when the unseen harmony which enables us to differ passionately on the most trivial matters with no loss of mutual esteem, becomes happily apparent; an amicable impulse of gravitation sets us moving towards a common goal. On your eightieth birthday, Master, we unite in offering you a token of affectionate regard. We recall with pride that you were a leader among those pioneers whose imagination has opened an immeasurable vista beneath the bounds of human sight, and has read in the dust of earth the secrets of the stars. Your name will stand with those few who have enhanced the peculiar fame bequeathed to our society by Newton. No less than by your achievements in the pursuit of learning, you have deserved well of the College by your unfailing interest in every one of its activities and by your patient and impartial kindliness in presiding over our deliberations.

Together with your family and other friends we wish that your days may be prolonged in the enjoyment of good will and honour, with peace of mind.

D. A. WINSTANLEY, *Vice-Master*	J. BURNABY	G. H. HARDY[c]
	H. F. STEWART	S. RUNCIMAN[d]
A. F. KIRKPATRICK	RUTHERFORD[abc]	W. S. FARREN[c]
J. G. FRAZER[acd]	G. I. TAYLOR[ac]	A. H. WILSON[c]
J. D. DUFF	T. C. NICHOLAS	P. RICHARDS
A. N. WHITEHEAD[acd]	F. W. ASTON[bc]	E. F. WARBURG
W. C. D. DAMPIER[c]	G. P. LENOX-	S. CHANDRASEKHAR[c]
J. W. CAPSTICK	CONYNGHAM[c]	M. BLACK
H. MCLEOD INNES	G. KITSON CLARK	C. J. HAMSON
F. M. CORNFORD[d]	C. D. BROAD[d]	C. A. COULSON[c]
E. HARRISON	F. J. W. ROUGHTON[c]	D. E. LEA
G. LAPSLEY	W. R. DEAN	J. E. POWELL
F. J. DYKES	G. E. MOORE[ad]	H. HEILBRONN[c]
A. S. EDDINGTON[ac]	A. S. F. GOW[d]	J. WISDOM
J. E. LITTLEWOOD[c]	P. W. DUFF	H. C. GILSON
H. F. NEWALL[c]	R. A. NICHOLSON[d]	V. ROTHSCHILD[c]
H. A. HOLLOND	R. M. RATTENBURY	D. A. G. HINKS
D. S. ROBERTSON[d]	G. M. TREVELYAN[acd]	H. W. MELVILLE[c]
F. GOWLAND HOPKINS[abc]	F. H. SANDBACH[d]	N. FEATHER[c]
F. A. SIMPSON	N. A. de BRUYNE[c]	M. H. L. PRYCE[c]
F. R. TENNANT[d]	C. F. A. PANTIN[c]	A. DALE TRENDALL[d]
J. R. M. BUTLER	H. O. EVENNETT	A. L. HODGKIN[abc]
E. D. ADRIAN[abc]	A. H. J. KNIGHT	T. T. PATERSON
R. H. FOWLER[c]	A. S. BESICOVITCH[c]	
D. H. ROBERTSON[d]	F. G. MANN[c]	

18 December 1936

[a] Order of Merit [b] Nobel Prize [c] Fellow of the Royal Society [d] Fellow of the British Academy

In retrospect, it may be hard to realize the awe in which the young Fellows held the older ones. Whitehead, Eddington, Littlewood, Gowland Hopkins, Adrian, Fowler, Rutherford,

Taylor, Aston, Broad, Moore, Trevelyan, Hardy and Coulson, to mention a few, were enough to subdue even the most ebullient. To this day and in spite of Rab, the kindest and wittiest of friends, I have not conquered my fear of the high table at Trinity.

Looking back on my scientific career, I believe I had one original idea which is now of no consequence, and investigated a few, but only a few, subjects which in retrospect do not seem pedestrian. The original idea was prompted by a footnote to an article in the scientific journal *Nature* by the distinguished astrophysicist and Fellow of Trinity, Chandrasekhar. He said that if you looked out of the window and at regular intervals counted the number of pedestrians walking along a particular, known length of pavement, you could deduce from the counts the average speed at which the pedestrians were walking. Scientists had long wondered how to measure the speed at which sperm swim; and it occurred to me that Chandrasekhar's footnote might provide an answer, if it was possible to translate his one-dimensional problem into two dimensions. All those mathematical supervisions during World War II, to which I refer later, helped me to achieve this objective.

I had another interesting idea, but again I am not sure where it led. In most animals only one sperm fertilizes an egg, prompting the question of what stops the other sperm from doing the same. It occurred to me that light might be shed on this problem by treating an egg in a suspension of sperm as if it were a sphere being bombarded by gas molecules. This led to a quite interesting series of experiments and published papers in collaboration with the present Chairman of the BBC, Sir Michael Swann, FRS. The reader may be surprised that this book compresses twenty-five years of intensive research into the two preceding paragraphs and a snippet on pages 39-40. But I owe it to the layman to spare him a long chapter in my life that can only be written in technical language. How captivated, I wonder, would the common reader be by a discourse on the Rheotaxis of Spermatozoa?[3] I have therefore contented myself with the one in two thousand chance of slicing a just-fertilized sea-urchin egg in such a way that the whole length of the sperm head can be seen inside the egg (opposite page 40).

I had one success which eludes many scientists: to know when to stop. At the age of forty-eight I realized that though I could continue, with assistance, to do quite interesting experiments and knew how to present the results in a way which ensured their publication, my work was becoming monotonous and not too interesting. I therefore decided to stop.

While I was still an active scientist, Lord Addison, Lord President of the Council in the Attlee Government, invited me to become Chairman of the Agricultural Research Council (ARC), a part-time post I held for ten years. In those days it was normal for the Secretary of a Research Council to be a good or eminent scientist and the Chairman a layman. Now the position was reversed. I was considered a reasonably good scientist, whereas the Secretary, Sir William Slater, had given up science at an early age. This atypical partnership had no ill effects, Sir William Slater and I working harmoniously together for nearly ten years. He used to say he did not like cold water but that when I pushed him in, he was a strong swimmer.

When I took over the Chairmanship of the ARC it was a very poor relation of the Medical Research Council and I felt that my most important function was to up-grade the ARC's scientific reputation. I hope my efforts were not unsuccessful. What I did not succeed in doing, in spite of the guidance and efforts of Solly Zuckerman, at that time a member of the ARC, was to inculcate into the ARC's Institutes a more positive sense of the agricultural needs of the nation as opposed to the local industry they served. We were not helped by the attitude at that time of the Ministry of Agriculture, which positively forbade the ARC having anything to do with agricultural economics. That, the Ministry said, was their affair and that of their Agricultural Improvement Council on which we were represented, but which seemed to us a sterile, paper-producing body. Even Solly did not have the power to rectify the extraordinary aberration whereby those concerned with research were not allowed to be concerned, centrally at any rate, with the value or otherwise of their products to the nation.

I mentioned earlier that the ARC was, in terms of prestige, a poor relation of the Medical Research Council. The inferior status of at least some of those concerned with agriculture had not disappeared even a very few years ago; agricultural economists in Whitehall were paid less than other economists in the Government's Economic Service. One is entitled to ask why, given that we have to grow half our food and that the fall in the value of sterling during the last few years has swollen our food import bill astronomically.

My life in World War II was divided into two parts, mathematics and anti-sabotage. When it became clear that the war would preclude me from continuing with my biophysical work I called on the great mathematician G. H. Hardy in Trinity College, Cambridge and said to him: 'I want to learn advanced mathematics. How should I set about it?'. He asked me a few questions, as a result of which he said: 'You have the mathematical ability of an intelligent schoolboy aged fourteen. As you are going to be in London most of the time, I will get into touch with a friend of mine, Professor Hyman Levy of Imperial College, and tell him about you. Call on him in about a week, but ensure that you are not taught by someone too clever.' As a result, for more than five years I had almost weekly supervisions or tutorials in advanced mathematics, with examples to be done in between. Doing examples at my age was salutary – but hard work. Re-reading my notebook, I find I got as far as Orthogonal Bessel Functions but became confused and dispirited by Poles and Residues.

Anti-sabotage consisted first, of identifying key points in the United Kingdom and elsewhere to be protected against enemy saboteurs; and secondly, of dismantling sabotage bombs which were invariably camouflaged as something else. Some details about these bombs will be found in Chapter 3: an episode involving a crate of onions from Spain which ended their life near Northampton.

By far the most difficult task was to protect Winston Churchill. Apart from the obvious pleasure he derived from personal danger, Winston was continually receiving cigars from all over the world. It seemed too easy to coat the proximal end of one of them with cyanide or better (in one sense) *botulinus* toxin; or to put inside one cigar a small high explosive charge activated by the heat of lighting the distal end. Accordingly, it was agreed by the 'authorities' that Winston's cigars should be sent to me for examination. A statistical technique was worked out in consultation with Lord Cherwell. Dr Bruce White, of the Medical Research Council, did the necessary experimental work after the cigars had been X-rayed. I told the Prime Minister that some of his cigars were ground up in saline, injected into mice and, according to their reactions, he got the cigars or he did not. He was amused by the experiments but displeased by any delay. I would then receive irate messages.

Cigars were not the only trouble. On one occasion, when walking across Parliament Square to the House of Commons, the Prime Minister was accosted by a French General who saluted and presented him with a Virginia ham. This greatly pleased Winston who remarked that he would have it for breakfast the next morning. There was panic. How could the ham be tested without his knowing and be ready for breakfast the next morning? An intricate surgical operation was undertaken whereby a very thin slice of ham was removed without disturbing the ham's surface. What could be done with the slice, time being far too short for bacteriological examination? After a high pressure conference a solution was, as usual, found. The slice of ham was fed to the Medical Research Council cat which was kept under minute examination for many hours. As it survived, the Prime Minister had his Virginia ham for breakfast the next morning.

Something similar happened when, in 1944, Winston went to France to visit de Gaulle and was presented by an admirer with twelve bottles of 1798 Armagnac. I felt it essential for the donor to produce a thirteenth bottle (for testing), which my colleagues and I sampled with pleasure. After that the Prime Minister was allowed to have the other twelve.

The rest of my life, with the exception of my private life which is my private property, is the subject of this book.

2

ASSASSINATION OF
A DIPLOMAT

The Times, 12 December 1938

On 7 November 1938 Herr von Roth, Third Secretary at the German Embassy in Paris, and nephew of Herr Koester, a former German Ambassador in Paris, was seriously wounded by several revolver shots. His assailant was a seventeen-year-old Polish Jew, Herschel Reibel Grynsban, who managed to get into the German Embassy by saying he had important documents to give to the Ambassador's secretary.

Grynsban submitted quietly to arrest and said that he had wished to avenge his co-religionists who were being persecuted under National Socialist rule and, in particular, Polish Jews who had recently been expelled from Germany. A fortnight before the attack he had received a letter from his parents describing their sufferings after being expelled from Germany.

Herr von Roth died and his murder was made the excuse for bestial attacks by the authorities on Jews in Germany and Austria.

On 9 November Jewish cultural life was virtually brought to a standstill. Their national and local newspapers and magazines were shut down, thus cutting the Jews off from their only sources of information, not only about Jewish cultural activities but about emigration.

On 10 November the Jews of Germany and Austria were subjected (still in the name of reprisal) to an organized campaign of plunder, destruction and violence. Synagogues were burnt, Jewish-owned shops were looted and Jews were attacked. The attacks were led by young Nazis and the Hitler Youth. Goebbels depicted the violence as a spontaneous outburst and urged people to leave the reprisals to the authorities. But, in fact, it was plain to everybody that they had been carefully planned.

*

SIR,

May I remind your readers of two points concerning yesterday's pogroms in Germany:

(1) Some people may think, from reading the newspapers,

27

that pogroms are something new in the treatment of the Jews in Germany. That is untrue. The difference between the treatment of the Jews during the last three or four days and their treatment during the last three or four years is quantitative. Qualitatively, these things have been going on continuously.

(2) The reports from Germany that the pogroms are 'spontaneous demonstrations' by the German people are a terrible defamation of the character of the German people as a whole. The German people are very much like the British. They detest the persecution of innocent people. I have received letters from Germany, from Germans who are not Jews and not even 'liberals'; from people who sympathize with the Nazi régime. But they have told me that they abhor the persecution of the Jews just as much as they and we abhor the beating up of Cardinal Innitzer or the 'protective detention' of a brave and good man, Pastor Niemöller.

It has been announced in the newspapers that any criticisms made in foreign countries of the treatment of the Jews will only increase their torments in Germany. I have no fear of doing this, because their torments cannot be increased except by such refinements of torture as would create general horror in Germany itself. Almost the only thing left for them is death; for many that would be a welcome and blessed relief.

May I add that, like Mr Laski and Mr Montefiore, I deeply deplore and condemn the assassination of the Third Secretary to the German Embassy in Paris. The Polish boy who did this was not in a condition to appreciate what he was doing. He was mad. Your readers will doubtless know why.

Yours faithfully,

ROTHSCHILD

3

EXAMINATION OF A CRATE OF ONIONS NEAR NORTHAMPTON

A Field Telephone Conversation, 10 February 1944

The recipient of the Field Telephone Conversation, for obvious reasons a considerable distance away, was Miss Cynthia Shaw, later Mrs Fulton. The technique of tele-dictation was not original.

＊

'IT IS a crate in three compartments. The right-hand compartment has onions in it. The middle compartment also appears to have onions in it. The left-hand compartment has already had most of the onions taken out but I can see right at the bottom in the left-hand corner of the left-hand compartment one characteristic block of German TNT. Next to it is some material which looks rather like plastic explosive and in that there is a hole in one bit which is about the size that a detonator would need. It might be plastic explosive or it might be something which is to keep the bricks of TNT in position. I am now going to stop talking and start taking onions out. I am going to start with the middle compartment to see what there is below the onions there.

I can now see one block of TNT in the middle compartment, top left-hand side.

I can now see another block of TNT in the middle compartment, top right-hand side.

There are no TNT blocks in what I might call the bottom centre compartment. By 'bottom' I mean the side nearest to me; by top I mean the side furthest away from me. There is no TNT on the side nearest to me. I am still on the middle. I am now going to see if there is any in the middle of the middle compartment.

I cannot find more than two blocks in the middle compartment. I am not certain about that yet, but I cannot find more than two. I am now going to go to the right-hand compartment because I am looking for the delay mechanism or initiating device. There does not seem room for it in the middle compartment, but I am having difficulty in the middle compartment because the onions have grown and are difficult to pull out.

I think I can see some of that plastic substance in the right-hand top edge, that is, the far away side of the right-hand compartment. I can just see it and I am now going to go on taking out some onions above it.

I have come to a block of TNT in the right-hand compartment, furthest side away from me to the left of the right-hand compartment. There is a sort of putty-like thing next to it. I am not sure what that is. I am going back to the extreme left-hand compartment because I want to try and get as much TNT out as I can.

I have now taken all the onions out of the left-hand compartment. There remains a cast block of TNT and a big bit of this putty-like substance. The volume of the putty-like substance is about the same as that of the cast brick. I cannot see any detonating fuse yet. I am now going very gently to take out the cast brick of high explosive.

I have taken out that and a few little bits of this putty-like material. I am now going to try and take this putty-like material out. There is something at the right-hand end which looks a little like a bit of tape.

I have taken that out and I am now going to start doing the same on the centre compartment.

There are only two bricks of TNT in the centre compartment.

I am now going to try and take out these two bricks of TNT. I shall start with the left-hand one. It seems to be a little loose.

I have taken out the left-hand block of TNT.

I have taken out the right-hand block of TNT. I am now going to go back to the right-hand compartment. The delay mechanism and detonator must be in that compartment and I am going to start slowly taking the onions away again.

I can now see a cast block of TNT, top left-hand side of right-hand compartment, at the furthest side away across the compartment. On its right, filling up the rest of the space to the right-hand end of the compartment is a chunk of that plastic material. I still cannot see any delay. I am having difficulty because the onions are jammed right in and I do not want to pull hard.

Crate of onions before bomb was removed, showing one block of high explosive, plastic high explosive and onions.

Block of cast high explosive and piece of plastic high explosive.

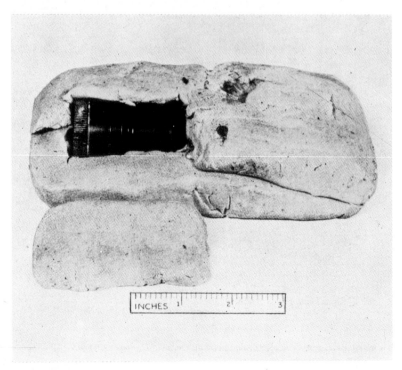

Plastic high explosive partially opened, showing 21-day German time clock embedded in it.

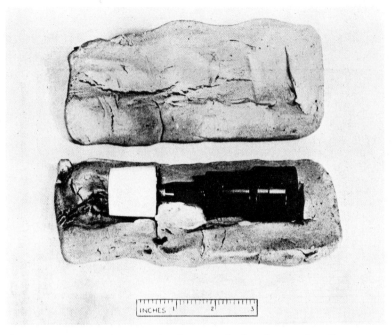

Plastic high explosive completely opened, showing 21-day German
time clock with detonator inserted in high explosive primer.

21-day German time clock showing adjustable dial calibrated
in days up to 21.

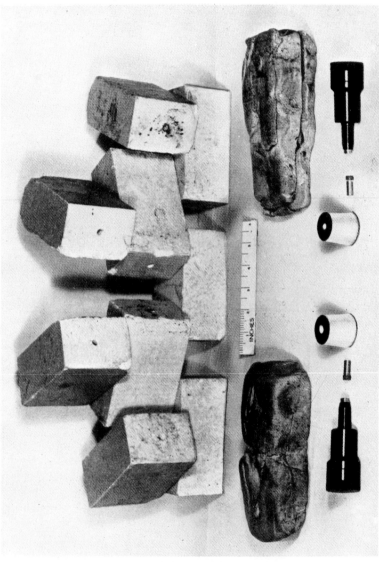

Nine of the ten blocks of high explosive, two pieces of plastic high explosive, two 21-day German time clocks, two detonators, and two primers.

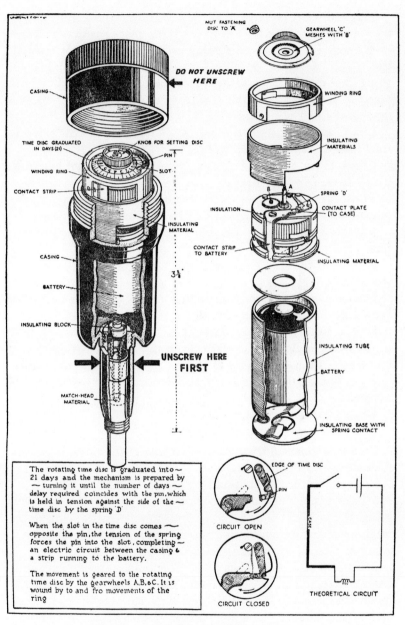

NUT FASTENING
DISC TO 'A'

GEARWHEEL 'C'
MESHES WITH 'B'

**DO NOT UNSCREW
HERE**

CASING

WINDING RING

INSULATING
MATERIALS

TIME DISC GRADUATED
IN DAYS (21)

KNOB FOR SETTING DISC

PIN

WINDING RING

SLOT

CONTACT STRIP

INSULATION

SPRING 'D'

CONTACT PLATE
(TO CASE)

INSULATING
MATERIAL

CONTACT STRIP
TO BATTERY

CASING

INSULATING MATERIAL

BATTERY

$3\frac{3}{4}$

INSULATING BLOCK

INSULATING TUBE

BATTERY

**UNSCREW HERE
FIRST**

MATCH-HEAD
MATERIAL

INSULATING BASE WITH
SPRING CONTACT

The rotating time disc is graduated into ~
21 days and the mechanism is prepared by
~ turning it until the number of days ~
delay required coincides with the pin, which
is held in tension against the side of the ~
time disc by the spring 'D'

When the slot in the time disc comes ~
opposite the pin, the tension of the spring
forces the pin into the slot, completing ~
an electric circuit between the casing &
a strip running to the battery.

The movement is geared to the rotating
time disc by the gearwheels A, B, & C. It is
wound by to and fro movements of the
ring

EDGE OF TIME DISC

PIN

CIRCUIT OPEN

CASE

CIRCUIT CLOSED

THEORETICAL CIRCUIT

Diagram of 21-day German time clock
(by Laurence Fish)

This is the last block of TNT that I can see and I am going to try very gently to move it away from the plastic with which it is in contact. I do not see the delay or the time clock. It must be inside the plastic or possibly buried underneath it, and I am going very gently to try and get this block of TNT out, but I am going to take a little of the plastic away first to see if there is a detonator sticking into the hole in the block of TNT.

I have taken out the last block of TNT and I am now going to start looking at the plastic explosive.

I have taken out the plastic explosive but I have not looked at it yet. It seems rather heavy.

There is nothing else in the crate now and I am going to bring out the blocks of TNT and then go back to look at the plastic.

I am now going to start trying to take this plastic explosive to pieces.

I see a primer inside one of them. I am going to try and take that out.

I have taken the primer out and I can now see the detonator buried in the middle of the plastic.

It is a twenty-one-day Mark II German time clock. I have unscrewed the electric detonator from the Mark II delay so that one is safe. I am now going to look at the other piece of plastic.

I can just see the other Mark II delay inside the other piece of plastic.

I have taken the other primer off.

The other detonator is off.

All over, all safe now.'

4

THE SITUATION IN PALESTINE

The House of Lords, 31 July 1946

On that day the House of Lords debated the 'Situation in Palestine' and Lord Addison, Secretary of State for Dominion Affairs, reported the British Government's reactions to the recommendations made by The Anglo-American Commission of Inquiry into the Problems of European Jewry and Palestine. The Commission made a number of recommendations among which were the partition of Palestine into four areas and the right of entry, into a 'Jewish Province' in Palestine, of 100,000 Jews to be selected primarily from Germany, Austria and Italy.

The debate took place at a time when there was great unrest in Palestine and a few days after the blowing up of a large part of the King David Hotel in Jerusalem.

＊

MY LORDS, it is with considerable embarrassment that I speak on the subject of today's Motion. I am embarrassed because it was only a few months ago that I was a British Army officer. During the war, even though one may not have been very near the front line, it was unfortunately a fairly commonplace occurrence to hear that one's fellow soldiers had been killed. But there is something dreadful about fellow soldiers being killed in time of peace, and no Jew, quite apart from those who were in the British Army, can fail to feel despair and shame when confronted with the stark fact that his co-religionists, who have traditionally abhorred war and violence, should have been responsible for the deaths of British soldiers. It is also embarrassing for me to say something about the aspirations of the Jews in Palestine when, in fact, I do not entirely share those aspirations. Nevertheless, I feel impelled to say something about the situation in Palestine from a point of view which almost by definition must be strange to nearly everyone in England.

I have noticed that it is customary for noble Lords, when they are speaking in certain debates, to make quite clear what is their personal position in regard to the subject under discussion. I should therefore like to say that I have never been a supporter of Zionism, or what is called political Zionism; nor have I been connected officially or unofficially with any Zionist organization.

It would be a waste of your Lordships' time to go over the old ground again; for me to try and interpret the Balfour Declaration or Sir Henry MacMahon's letter, which is said by some to contradict the Balfour Declaration; or to go into the history of Palestine – who got there first; who 'kicked' who out, and so on. Such matters have often been discussed before by your Lordships, and in any case there are great authorities in this House on that subject. I need only refer to the noble Viscount, the Leader of the Opposition, and the noble Viscount, the Leader of the Liberal Party, who have already spoken. I should, however, like to say a few words to your Lordships about something rather strange to all of us; that is, the mentality of the Jews in Palestine and the causes of that mentality.

When I put before you their reactions and their interpretation of the Palestine situation, I think it is necessary to remember two basic facts which have had a profound effect on the Jewish mentality. First, whatever the reasons, there are few countries in the world where the Jews have not been harried or persecuted for many hundreds of years. Even in 1946, pogroms go on in Europe – I refer to the one at Kielce in Poland in July – pogroms based on the old, old story of the Jews murdering Christian children. And Cardinals, in spite of the precepts of many Popes, refuse to condemn such acts, even when the person who invented the story has admitted that it was a lie.

The second basic fact is that almost all the young Jews in Palestine have had fathers, mothers, and relations who were among the six million Jews tortured and gassed to death by Hitler. It is a strange feeling to have had relations put to death in some terrible way. I wonder how many of your Lordships are in the same position that I am, of having had an aunt whom one loved dearly – she was seventy-five years old and quite blind – clubbed to death by the SS on the railway station outside an extermination camp. She had kept a small farm in Hungary for many years, and was much liked by the other farmers in the district. Please do not think that by telling this story I am trying to evoke any personal sympathy. I tell it quite objectively, because I believe such episodes help one to understand the despair and desperation which have led to the unforgettable events of the last few months. When such things happen to people without the advantages we have in England, the results are terrible and the wounds may take long to heal. They need all the understanding and forgiveness of which we are capable, however sorely tried we may be.

But there was more to be superimposed on this intolerable suffering. There was the White Paper. Many Jews felt that it was a betrayal of previous promises. Some were doubtful about their interpretation of these promises and thought they might be biased and illogical, but they were fortified in their beliefs by no less a person than Winston Churchill who said, referring to certain parts of this White Paper:

'That is a plain breach of a solemn obligation, a breach of faith . . . What will those who have been stirring up these Arab agitators think? Will they not be tempted to say, "They are on the run again. This is another Munich".'

Naturally, this did not influence any Jew, Zionist or non-Zionist, when the war came; they fought, died, and shed their blood like all other democratic people. But the Palestine Jews could not help but notice the Arab record during the war; the Rashid Ali rebellion in Iraq, in which a member of the Irgun lost his life while on a special mission for the British. He is now a captain – in the Habbaniyah cemetery. Nor can they forget the Egyptian Minister of Defence who, in 1941, delivered the defence plans for Egypt to the Axis. They cannot help noticing that the Mufti, quite commonly known in the war as an agent of Hitler – and your Lordships will remember that the Mufti trained the Bosnian SS, and for that reason was at one time wanted as a war criminal by another country – is an honoured guest of a King who has always expressed his sympathies with the Arab cause, and a King in whose country bomb outrages in which British soldiers have been killed are by no means unknown.

Finally, we come to the recent Anglo-American Committee and its recommendations. The Committee recommended that 100,000 Jews should be allowed to enter Palestine. A prerequisite of this recommendation being implemented was that no further acts of terrorism should take place. The Government added what at any rate appeared to be a further condition, that illegal armies in Palestine should all disarm before these displaced people were allowed into Palestine. The Jews, constrained in Palestine, felt, quite wrongly no doubt, that this added condition was directed against them, rather than against the Arabs, who had all the surrounding countries, such as Transjordan and Syria, in which to prepare for resistance. They remembered that one of the reasons for their being armed was to guard themselves against attacks by the Arabs on their communal settlements – attacks which the British authorities admitted they could not prevent. This Jewish Army, the members of which, as your Lordships know, did many acts of valour for England during the war, was actually trained by a national hero of ours, General Wingate. The Haganah became powerful at a time when Jewish settlements were being ruthlessly attacked and pillaged by the Arabs, who have quite recently announced their intention of resisting by force any immigration into Palestine, just as they did before when they were responsible for the growth of this Jewish Army.

In this country, the idea of any organization having an Army of its own is inconceivable. But it is not easy for us to understand the life of someone in a communal settlement in Palestine, where at any moment he may be the victim of a savage and murderous attack. These communal settlements have a special place in Jewish life. How often have we all heard that the Jews do not work with their hands, cannot till the soil, and are destined for ever to be urban dwellers engaged in small urban business? Palestine, for whatever the reason, is the only country where the Jews, after 2000 years, have been able to get back to their business of tilling the soil and living on the land. Can we put ourselves in their position and realize what it means, having at last settled down in what they believe to be the Promised Land, when their fields are burnt and ravaged by gangs of marauding Arabs, while they are utterly unable to defend themselves?

These factors, extermination in Europe during the war, pogroms in Europe after it, and what they believe to be discrimination against them in Palestine, have produced absolute despair and absolute desperation. Now what sort of person is it who has these suicidal feelings? Perhaps this story may give an indication. During the war my work took me into a house in France where there had been an explosion. I learnt there about a Jewish member of the Resistance Movement who was arrested by the Gestapo and asked to give certain information about the whereabouts and names of his colleagues. He, of course, refused. The flesh on his arms, near his shoulders, was carefully cut round with razor blades and the whole skin peeled off as if it were gloves or sticking plaster. The same was then done to his legs. He refused to give any names. He was bricked up in a wall for forty-eight hours and, on being taken out, was suspended from the ceiling by his wrists with weights attached to his body.* He still refused to give the names of his colleagues. He was then sent to an extermination camp and by some ironical miracle escaped, to be mercifully killed in the explosion which I investigated. The courage of that man is difficult to appreciate in the comparative security of England.

How fortunate it is that human beings find it so difficult to appreciate the horrors and miseries that go on in the world. We hear that millions of Indians have starved to death, or that countless Chinese have been drowned in floods. We say, and even perhaps feel for a short time, 'How terrible', and then we go about our business. It is lucky that we can do this because if we could really feel what has happened we should perhaps be unable to go on living. The same applies about the Jew who was skinned alive, or his six million co-religionists who were gassed, tortured, and experimented on by Hitler. We say 'How terrible', then we forget and go about our business. But, and this is the thing I find so difficult to keep in my mind, not one Jew in Palestine forgets one of these episodes – forgets that the woman in the next settlement had her one-year-old daughter roasted alive in front of her eyes. And when the scales seemed once more to be weighted against them, the last tenuous threads snapped and they said: 'There is no hope; therefore let us die fighting.'

I believe and pray that the Government's proposals, which we have heard today, may eventually produce a new state of mind in Palestine and hope, given some goodwill and moderation on both sides. I said at the beginning that I would try and explain

* This is a euphemism.

37

to your Lordships the state of mind which has produced the recent events in Palestine. With the many advantages that I have, it is comparatively easy for me to say that I do not entirely share the aspirations of the Jews in Palestine. I am thinking not so much of the material ones as the advantage of being accepted as an Englishman. But even I remember that only a few years ago my grandfather was the first Jew your Lordships allowed to sit in this House, and I therefore felt it my duty to try and explain something of the trials and torments of my co-religionists in Palestine.

5

THE FERTILIZING
SPERMATOZOON

An article in *Discovery*, 1957[4]

Fertilizin, referred to in this article, is a chemical excreted by
some unfertilized eggs. 1 Ångstrom is about four billionths of an
inch. The reader must, I am afraid, consult the technical literature
if he or she is interested in the meaning of the technical words
at the end of the article.[5,6]

*

MANY fertilization studies are carried out on sea-urchins,
because their eggs and spermatozoa are easy to obtain in great
numbers. Unfortunately, sea-urchin spermatozoa are smaller
than those of mammals, which makes it almost impossible to see
in any detail what changes take place in them after fertilization.
Apart from this, small structures are difficult to identify within an
intact egg and it is therefore necessary to cut the egg into thin
slices or sections to get the best out of the microscope with which
it is being examined.

The sea-urchin spermatozoon can enter the egg anywhere on
its surface; one section of the egg is, for this reason, unlikely to
contain the minute spermatozoon for which one is looking; and
even if it does, the section may well not pass through the spermatozoon at a convenient angle.

These observations apply to examination with the light
microscope. Matters become even more difficult when an attempt
is made to take advantage of the magnification and resolution
possible with the electron microscope, the only instrument with
which the fine structure of a spermatozoon can be seen. To
achieve good resolution, sections must be not more than about
400 Ångstroms thick. As a sea-urchin egg is 1 million Ångstroms
in diameter, more than 2000 sections would have to be cut per
egg and kept for examination – an almost impossible task – to be
certain of finding the fertilizing spermatozoon in a section suitable

for electron microscopy. Even then, as mentioned above, the plane of the section might well be such as to make the spermatozoon difficult to identify or reconstruct. To find out what effect fertilizin has on the spermatozoon, one must cut longitudinal sections of the spermatozoon before fertilization, similar to those obtained by Afzelius[7] and Rothschild[8]; but this was an easier task because for every spermatozoon inside an egg, there can be 5000 available for section-cutting when the sperm are in their prefertilization environment.

My assistant Mr J. N. Thomson and I have obtained two sections of just-fertilized sea-urchin eggs, in which the planes of the sections were such that the fertilizing spermatozoa were approximately in longitudinal section (see opposite). As this improbable event may not have been achieved before, the electron micrographs of these sea-urchin spermatozoa, three minutes after fertilization, may be of interest.

Bearing in mind the dangers of generalizing from isolated electron micrographs, the following changes in the appearance of the fertilizing spermatozoon may be worthy of mention:

(1) Except in the region of the centriole, the nuclear membrane seems to have 'dissolved'.

(2) The centriole is double or has divided into two. (At some stage after fertilization the centriole must divide into two.)

(3) The sperm tail, terminating at the posterior end of the centriole, is clearly visible within the egg cytoplasm.

(4) The middle-piece looks quite different after fertilization. It is larger and more symmetrical, while its membrane is crinkly and discontinuous.

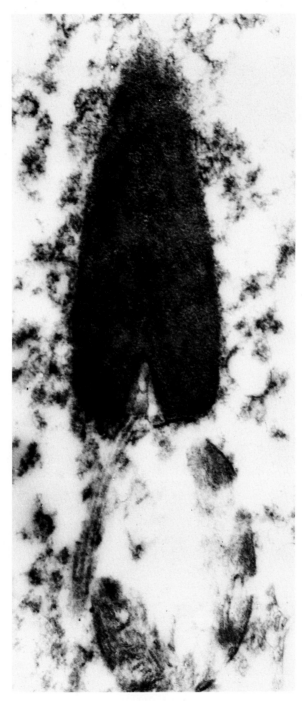

Electron micrograph of the head, middle piece (lower half right) and part of the tail (lower half left) of a sea-urchin spermatozoon, three minutes after fertilising a sea-urchin egg. The spermatozoon is inside the egg. (x50,000)

6

SCIENCE IN INDUSTRY

Address to the Imperial Defence College, 4 April 1968

THE title of this talk is 'Science in Industry'; but I must start by explaining that I am only qualified to discuss science and, in particular, research and development, in *one* industry, the Royal Dutch-Shell Group.

Before joining Shell I was a Don at Cambridge University engaged in biophysical research, but during that time I had, for ten years, a part-time job, which took about one and a half days a week, as Chairman of the Agricultural Research Council, which actually is a small Government Department. I knew very little about agriculture or agricultural research, but was familiar with scientific language and the methods of research, points to which I shall revert later.

With this history, I am fairly well placed to compare Government, academic and industrial research and development and it may be of interest to you to hear some impressions, at times critical, of the differences, inevitable or unnecessary, between these three activities.

A moment or two ago you may have gained the impression that only to have been concerned with science in one industry is a disadvantage. This may not be serious if the one industry is Shell because of the immense diversity of its technological activities. Many people, including some who should know better, imagine that Shell is almost wholly concerned with finding oil, getting it out of the ground or from under the sea, putting it into something called a refinery which produces petrol and lubricating oil, and putting these products into motor cars, aeroplanes and the like. In fact, Shell is one of the twelve largest chemical companies in the world and though oil, as found below the surface of the earth, is one of the most versatile starting materials for all chemical processes, we are by no means wedded to it in our chemical business.

There are very few scientific disciplines in which a company such as Shell is not interested. Astrophysics is one though we are interested in travel in outer space, both because of the propulsion and lubrication of space-craft; organ transplantation, about which we thought before the public heard of Dr Barnard, is another. But we have, for example, found it necessary to hire very rarified and unexpected types, such as topologists, who work on a subject normally considered to be of extreme purity. I shall come back later to the width of our activities.

The word 'purity' as applied to science prompts me to digress for a few minutes about those over-used and so often misunderstood words, pure and applied science. Talleyrand said that treason was largely a matter of dates: a hero in 1917, Trotsky for example in Russia, may well be a traitor a few years later; and indeed, judging by the fact that Stalin had Trotsky bumped off in 1940 with an icepick in Mexico, this was the case, at any rate so far as Russia was concerned. So it is with research. Nobody in their senses at Cambridge believed Rutherford's experiments on atom-splitting could have any of the applications with which we are now painfully or pleasurably familiar. At the time the great British scientist J. B. S. Haldane recorded in print that there was no possibility of using radioactivity as a source of power; he said he had made some thermodynamic calculations, which no one has actually seen, which made this obvious.

But apart from considerations of dates, there is another way in which pure and applied science become inextricably confused with each other and one which I quite often notice in Shell, as I did at Cambridge University. The actual research worker may himself be convinced that he is engaged in fundamental research; but his Director may have different ideas and see a possible application of his work. Let me give two examples. There is a man at one of Shell's Laboratories who researches on the structure and composition of extremely small crystalline bodies found inside certain bacteria. This is the work he was doing before joining Shell and which he is continuing. He considers it to be fundamental research and quite often says so. However, these crystalline bodies have a very interesting property. They are highly poisonous to insects and only particular kinds of insects. In addition they are harmless to man. To me, this scientist's work is, obviously, long-term applied research; to him it is fundamental.

Another example concerns myself. I used to work on the physiology of spermatozoa and, because of the tedium of filming them down a microscope to measure how fast they swam, I invented an electrical method of measuring their activity. Somewhat to my surprise this method became known in the world of artificial insemination where it has been used to measure the goodness or otherwise of bull semen. My motives for doing this work were entirely pure; but my Professor might well have twigged the possibility of a practical application.

Of course, at the elementary level, it is easy to make a distinction between pure and applied research. The former involves the pursuit of new knowledge for its own sake – what, for example, is the nature of the electrical message from the brain which tells my biceps to contract? Applied research has a practical objective – a new vaccine or an electrically-powered motor car. But in terms of how a person behaves in a laboratory, these distinctions are very fuzzy and not, to my mind, of great importance. You might counter these observations by saying 'fundamental research, the quest for new knowledge goes on indefinitely; surely applied research must have a time limit, if only because of competition in the market place? It is no good working on an electric car for years and years if others get there first. And in any case, can the company afford to spend money indefinitely on research which produces no results of commercial value?' This is a legitimate question, which I shall deal with in two parts: first, I am not at all sure that fundamental research should necessarily be allowed to go on indefinitely; nor am I sure that all fundamental research projects should be undertaken. I have known people at Cambridge University and elsewhere research on the same subject for years and years with reasonable competence; but without getting anywhere interesting, either because the original question was poorly formulated or because, even if the question was well formulated, the answer or answers were of little interest in the advancement of human knowledge. You see, I don't believe that the acquisition of *any* information is a worthwhile activity and merits the designation knowledge. This seems to me to apply particularly in the United Kingdom at the present time when we are in trouble, whereas at the beginning of this century and in the previous one, we were richer, as America is now, and therefore

43

could afford to be more free and easy. Some people may think this a Fascist or Communist philosophy. If carried to extremes which would, of course, be undesirable and unnecessary, that might be true.

In industrial research one often finds gaps in scientific knowledge which is needed and which necessitates research of a kind indistinguishable from that done at a University. The result is that, in Shell, a considerable sum out of our annual R & D Budget, about £4,500,000, is spent each year on such research, which may be concerned with mathematics, catalysis, biochemistry, information theory or the properties of very large molecules. The only thing which differentiates this work from that at a University is that it is relevant to our business. Why not farm out such research to our hard-pressed Universities? The answer is that we often do – enlightened self-interest you might call it; but we have found that intimate geographical proximity is of great value between those engaged in such research and their colleagues who have clearly defined practical objectives.

I have been talking about the alleged differences between so-called pure and so-called applied research. A somewhat analogous confusion arises about the words research and development. The difference between research and development is two-fold; first, development costs ten times as much as research; secondly, and as a consequence, the probability of a development programme being successful must be much higher than the probability that a particular research programme will go well; because one should not spend the money needed for development without a high probability that the results will warrant application or commercialization.

When I first joined Shell, partly because I felt my research was in what might be called a competent rut, several of my Cambridge colleagues were quite contemptuous about a Don joining industry. This snobbish and superior attitude still exists at some of our Universities and, in spite of the efforts of the President of the Royal Society, Blackett, who has, I believe, talked to you during this series, it still exists in some parts of the Royal Society. This attitude has very serious disadvantages for England. It does not exist to anything like the same extent in Holland, where I spend a lot of my time, nor in Germany, nor in America. In all of these, the interchange of scientists between Universities and industry is more frequent and intimate than in the United Kingdom. Serious efforts are now being made to put this situation right; but the going is hard on both sides. The leisurely atmosphere of Cambridge University with its archaic administration – a sitter for the McKinsey Corporation – is difficult to reconcile with the tension and urgency of industry, which sometimes reminds me of England during World War II. Of course, some people at Universities bear too heavy a teaching load, that is to say they are overworked. But the difference in tempo is really striking. My daughter, who has just graduated at Oxford and is spending a postgraduate year at MIT, is amazed by the difference between Oxford and MIT in this respect.

The pace was fairly leisurely when I was concerned with Government research, admittedly a number of years ago. But I have no reason to believe things have greatly changed since then, though of course, Government administration is far better than that of Cambridge University.

In retrospect, I think that when I was concerned with Government research I too easily acquiesced in such propositions as 'We must find out all about the physiology of the most important farm animal, the cow' because I was still a University man and insulated from many realities. Now, if the Director of the Institute of Animal Physiology at Babraham near Cambridge were to say this to me, I would ask why? How long will it take to make a useful dent in the problem? What will it cost? If I got the answer 'One can never tell when research will produce interesting or useful results, nor what fall-out of an unexpected nature there will be from it', I would not be very enthusiastic about the original proposition and might even make some old-fashioned remarks. In recent years, for good but, I believe, mistaken reasons, there has been a tendency to do something worse than find out all about the physiology of the cow at Government research establishments. It is to invent research projects for institutes which, for one reason or another, are unable to fulfil the role for which they were originally set up. I have been told, for example, that the Royal Aircraft Establishment at Farnborough is researching on washing machines. We all know that Harwell is working on the desalting of sea water, atmospheric

45

pollution and, possibly, the quantitative evaluation of research projects. I believe that this sort of diversification, if that is the right word, is often ridiculous; and that when an institute has outlived the purposes for which it was originally intended, it, or parts of it, should be closed, or handed over to the industry concerned with the subject in question, assuming the industry is prepared to finance it for commercial reasons. Another example concerns the National Gas Turbine Research Establishment. It seems obvious to me that this should be part of Rolls-Royce or, if Rolls-Royce does not want it, the establishment should be closed.

This brings me to one point which I believe to be very important: it is, unfortunately, the case that people in all branches of life outlive the original useful purpose for which they were employed. This does not in any sense imply that they are useless in other activities; but it does imply that there must be machinery to move them or change their jobs. When I was Chairman of the Agricultural Research Council I remember we had a complete dud in our Head Office. The Permanent Secretary, his Deputy and I were all agreed, not in this case that he had outlived his usefulness, but that he was useless. Nevertheless there was no method of moving him anywhere else nor of firing him. This system is conducive to gross inefficiency. At the same time, I believe that both for material and moral reasons, one cannot ruthlessly fire people without regard to their feelings or circumstances. One has got to look after them – and well. At present, we can still do this in industry: but a Don at a University can hardly be got rid of unless he is caught with his fingers in the till or if he commits an act of indecency. To give an example, when I was at Cambridge University there was a psychology lecturer who invariably drank a bottle of whisky each morning before giving his nine o'clock lectures, for which he arrived more or less on all fours. It appeared that the Statutes of Cambridge University did not enable any action to be taken. Just to give a twist to the story, perhaps I ought to add that not all of his lectures were as bad as might have been expected in the circumstances.

The embarrassment, which exists in the United Kingdom, about moving from one job to another, is far less evident in the United States. It is not a disgrace to leave Shell and join Monsanto.

It is not a disgrace to leave the Government Service and enter Shell; nor is it a disgrace to go from industry to University and *vice versa*. This mobility of jobs, not geographical mobility which is another but important problem, is, I believe, of great importance if we are to make this country efficient. It is far more important than belly-aching about the brain drain.

I referred earlier to Government research institutes engaging in research and development on subjects which were never dreamt of when the institute was created. This brings me to questions of organization and it may be useful briefly to outline how research and development is controlled in the Royal Dutch-Shell Group. We have a number of separate but interdependent activities: Exploration and Production of oil and natural gas; Oil Processes, which is principally to do with refineries, though questions such as sulphur and chimney gases arise, because many sorts of crude oil contain sulphur; Oil Products are those with which you are all familiar – petrol, lubricating oil, diesel oil, residual oil for boilers, bitumen of which very many of our roads are made and jet engine fuels; Natural Gas refrigerated to liquid form at $-160°C$ in tankers, or in its gaseous form; Chemicals Products & Processes, about which I have already spoken; Marine Transportation, which refers to our huge tanker fleet with its immensely complicated operation; Information and Computer Services, which is self-explanatory; and General Research.

With the exception of General Research, to which I shall return later, the programmes and budgets are controlled by those segments of Shell concerned with the business aspects of the activities I have mentioned. We call these segments Functions. Each of these business segments or Functions is headed up by what we call a Coordinator, equivalent to a Vice-President in an American company. There is, therefore, a Marine Coordinator and he determines the tanker R & D programme and what he is prepared to pay for it in the light of the business for which he is accountable. Of course, the establishment of an R & D programme is preceded by discussions and, often, disagreements between the businessmen and the research workers. It is essential, therefore, for the businessmen to have people with research experience in their own organizations. Otherwise they would have great difficulty in conversing with the research workers, let alone

47

understanding them. Shell has many laboratories, twenty-four major ones in the world, and it is one of the Research Coordinator's responsibilities to decide where a particular R & D programme should be executed. This rarely presents difficulties because it is usually self-evident where the technical expertise is located. To give a concrete example, our laboratory at Delft in Holland is wholly concerned with plastics and elastomer R & D. Obviously, this laboratory would not be suitable for R & D on lubricating oil.

Shell's research organization is therefore in the position of a contractor who provides a service, together with estimates of what the work will cost. At the same time we apply to all the Functions a surcharge, which explains the category General Research. At the moment this surcharge is running at about £4.5m, 11% of our world-wide budget, in pre-devaluation sterling. General Research consists of fundamental research in an area relevant to the business but in which there are gaps which have not been filled at Universities or elsewhere and which may be unsuitable for farming out to Universities. It also includes a considerable amount of R & D on instrument design and on analytical methods. When a research programme is concerned with matters of interest to two or more segments of the business, it is classified as General for reasons of administrative convenience. An example is R & D on fuel cell-powered motor vehicles. This programme may be of interest to the Chemical Function because of the fuel used, for example methyl alcohol. It may also be of interest to an entirely different part of the Chemical Function, if the manufacture of fuel cells involves a large off-take of plastics. It will obviously also be of interest to those concerned with Oil Products because an electrical vehicle would compete with those with which we are all familiar. Such multifunctional research, as we call it, is better processed by one, rather than three Functions.

Finally we include within General Research projects for which, at their inception, there is no Function (or business segment) in Shell. A recent and typical example is protein from natural gas. In the current list of Functions there is at present none concerned with food. This might develop through the Agricultural Chemicals Division of the Chemical Function, but at present this Division, as its name implies, is wholly occupied with fertilizers, insecticides, weed-killers, fungicides and the like.

You will appreciate from what I have just said that General Research, for which the Research Coordinator is accountable, provides a means to undertake research for which the businessmen see no future. To give an example, in 1952, a predecessor of mine thought that a particular gadget might be of interest to Shell and therefore warranted study in one of our laboratories. The businessmen were not interested in it, but my predecessor was convinced of its future use and it was therefore studied under the General Research heading. It happened to be a very early computer.

In spite of formal control and accountability by the businessmen for all R & D programmes and budgets except General Research, we have, of course, built-in safety valves so that a laboratory can say to me that such and such a Function is being unreasonable, for example in wanting a lot of work done but not being prepared to pay enough, or in wanting suddenly to stop a programme which, given the inertia of all research institutions, can rarely be done at short notice. Although the different Functions vary a great deal in their attitude towards research, some being much more research conscious than others, I have not, during the last ten years, found any serious conflicts between my research organization and the businessmen. Of course, one of my duties is to see that there are no such conflicts.

What sort of research and development do the businessmen commission? I mentioned earlier that some people think that what is often called a major international oil company is mainly or only concerned with finding oil and natural gas, turning oil into petrol and lubricants in a refinery, and getting these products into motor cars, aircraft and the like. But Exploration R & D poses computer problems which tax IBM, ICT, Control Data, Elliott-Automation and General Electric to the utmost and even beyond. Exploration for oil and natural gas by seismic means, below the surface of the earth and often, nowadays, below the sea as well, involves studying the reflections and refraction of seismic waves by different geological strata and by water, and making inferences about these waves, both as regards the nature of the geological strata and the probability of their containing oil or natural gas. Computers have revolutionized such studies but one end point, though feasible, has not yet been reached. It is for the output of the computer to consist of precise geological profiles on the oscilloscope screen, the input being recorded waves from the underground explosions. Those of you with computer knowledge or who are computer specialists may realize that this is a feasible but formidable problem which is giving the specialists quite a few headaches.

One of my special favourites in the field of refinery research and development concerns the new chimney in our refinery at Pernis, outside Rotterdam. Many people may think a chimney is a very ordinary object, of little or no interest to the scientist, engineer or mathematician. They may even believe that the one under discussion is no different from that on top of a house, apart from being somewhat bigger. Nevertheless, when examined in a little detail, the chimney at Pernis is absorbing to many of those concerned with it. It dominates the landscape and, sometimes, even

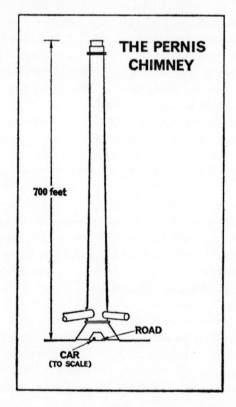

THE PERNIS
CHIMNEY

700 feet

ROAD

CAR
(TO SCALE)

one's thoughts. Of course its height, about 100 ft. taller than the GPO Tower in London, partly explains its fascination, as does the fact that a road passes through its base. But there are other reasons for the effect it has on those who see and study it. Why is it so big and tall? The refinery at Pernis produces a billion cubic feet of sulphur dioxide each year, which must not contaminate the village of Pernis, the neighbouring town of Rotterdam, nor even The Hague, which is relatively far off. The maximum desirable sulphur dioxide concentration at ground level is only 0.2 parts per million. How can this requirement be met on the occasions when the temperature of the air increases with height and a condition of extreme atmospheric stability, called inversion, occurs? The height of the chimney has to be such that the vast quantities of sulphur dioxide-containing gases are ejected well above the inversion layer. The flue gases come out of the top of the chimney at a rate of sixty million cubic feet an hour, at 45 miles per hour and, depending on the wind velocity, rise to as much as 1200 feet, nearly twice the height of the chimney.

These flue gases come to the chimney by ducts from twenty-five furnaces and thirteen boilers. The ducts are sixteen feet in diameter where they enter the chimney, so that there is enough room for a bus and a car to pass simultaneously along them. If the pressure in one furnace or boiler changes, adjustments have to be made to the pressures in all the other thirty-seven leading to the chimney. Were this to be done by human beings, thirty-eight operators would be continually engaged in adjusting pressures. To avoid this, the adjustments are done automatically by a machine which continually keeps all boiler and furnace pressures at the right level.

A severe operating problem and, perhaps, danger could arise from pressure fluctuations caused by atmospheric turbulence at the top of the chimney and from the resultant pressure amplification in the chimney and the ducts leading to it – acoustic gas resonance, as it is called. A mathematical analogue of the system was set up to determine the acoustic resonance frequencies under varying climatic conditions and this has permitted the specification of machines to control this undesirable phenomenon.

But there is another resonance problem which has to be eliminated. When there is a steady wind blowing, periodic vortex air shedding occurs on approximately the opposite sides of the chimney from which the wind blows. These vortices are not shed at the same time on each side, with the result that large periodic pressure changes can occur, making the chimney vibrate at a frequency of one cycle every four seconds, at right angles to the direction of the wind; this is the same principle as that which makes an Aeolian harp work. These pressure changes can produce a force equivalent to no less than 450 tons about 130 feet from the top of the chimney, with obvious results. To become a bit more technical for one moment, the problem to be overcome, therefore, is prevention of the laminar flow of air on the near side of the chimney and alteration of the vortex shedding on the other side. The normal way of doing this is to put what's called von Kármán spirals round the outside of the top of the chimney; but some uncertainty about the effects attainable with them led to a simpler and more certain solution. In order to induce turbulent air-flow all round the chimney and, therefore, prevent or average out the dangerously large pressure changes which might otherwise occur, concrete ribs have been put vertically on the top 200 feet of the chimney, at 10° intervals round its circumference.

From this description one can, I think, appreciate that an apparently simple object called a chimney is, in reality, complicated and interesting, not only because it dominates the scenery, but also because of the development problems its construction posed.

Research and development for the Marine Function may also be rather different from what some people might expect. We have of course studied bulbous bows on tankers; but in some ways seaweed on the hulls of tankers is more important because of what the increased drag caused by seaweed does to the tanker transportation bill. So far we have not solved this problem in Research, probably because we do not know how to tackle it.

Marine transportation also poses logistic problems of which the following is an example. It concerns the scheduling of tankers, that is, where they should go and when. There are about 130 different grades of oils to be dealt with, and the requirements for these have to be specified for individual discharge ports, of which there are some 350. These are supplied from 100 loading ports, arrival at the discharge ports being stipulated within certain date ranges. For the period immediately ahead, these requirements are fairly firm, but for the more distant future they can only be provisionally established. 450 tankers are available to be assigned to the required voyages, but of these, the only ones of interest are those which can reach the loading ports in time for the oil to arrive at the discharge ports within the agreed date ranges. Apart from the time factor, which restricts the number of possible assignments a tanker may have, there are other factors which may make a tanker unsuitable for a particular voyage, for example its size.

Having carried out its first assignment, a tanker will become available for a new one, at a point in time which will depend on the duration of the first voyage. If there are insufficient tankers to carry out all the required voyages, additional ones have to be chartered.

The problem is to *assign* individual tankers to particular voyages in such a way as to minimize ocean transportation costs, including the cost of chartering when this is necessary. It is not, of course, sufficient to minimize the cost of all 'first assignments'; their effect on the cost of future assignments must also be taken into consideration.

A further difficulty is that every day there are changes in the requirements-shipping data; suppose for example, our refinery at Petit-Couronne in France may have intended to take in 50,000 tons of a particular crude oil between certain dates, and the appropriate schedules were worked out. Nearer the dates in question there were problems at Petit-Couronne, a temporary shut-down for example, and the cargo, already on the way to France, had to be switched elsewhere at short notice. Such practical difficulties impose a severe limitation on the amount of time the computer can have to do the calculations if the results are to be of use.

A good part of such problems can be solved, but there still remain some features with which we cannot cope and which require more study.

We have also been doing research to increase the automation levels of tankers, particularly the very large ones, 200,000 tons and over, which are just coming into service. Automatic integrated bridge control systems are being developed for such tankers. The steam turbine plant of a tanker is simulated by an analogue computer in these studies which will lead to an automatic manoeuvring system that avoids low frequency instability and optimizes emergency stopping procedures. At the moment very large tankers tend to travel along a sinusoidal course – low frequency instability – instead of along a straight line. This wastes times, fuel and, therefore, money and interferes with emergency operations. The first of these automated bridge control systems has been fitted on a tanker belonging to the Deutsche Shell company. A more sophisticated version is in the process of being fitted on a tanker being built for us in Japan.

How does all this research and development go up to the top? It is here that such a vast organization as Shell differs from smaller companies, though not, perhaps, so much if one considers the Functions as separate companies which, of course, they are not, because earlier, I described them as being interdependent. The Shell Group is ruled by six Managing Directors to whom the Coordinators are accountable. In turn the Managing Directors are accountable to the Boards of Royal Dutch and Shell Transport & Trading, of which they are members. The Managing Director to whom I am accountable also has the following non-research responsibilities: Exploration & Production, Chemicals, our Central Offices organization and the administration of one of our two head offices, the one in The Hague. These duties, coupled with meetings of the Managing Directors' Committee twice or more a week and monthly Board meetings, necessitate a great deal of delegation to the Coordinators. In essence this is done by expenditure limits at various levels. Two Managing Directors can spend up to so much without reference to the Board, one up to so much, the Coordinator up to so much, and so on down the line. Within that framework each Coordinator is in charge of his part of the whole business.

In recent times there has been quite a lot of talk about the absence, in British companies, of scientists on the Boards. There is a good reason why there should be scientists or technically qualified people at the top of most organizations, not only companies. The reason is concerned with the need for speedy and comprehensible communication. Not only does it waste a tremendous amount of time to have to explain or justify decisions with a considerable technical content in completely lay language; but sometimes this may be impossible. That is why, to take an extreme example, books for the layman on quantum mechanics or relativity are confidence tricks. You thought you understood what it was all about, but I don't think you did. But there are two objections to having scientists right at the top of organizations, whether it be the Cabinet or a company. First, my experience is that, like everyone else, scientists are by no means likely to be proficient in branches of human activity other than their own. Nobel Prize-winners have, for example, been Members of Parliament and failed in this role. However desirable it may be for the scientist to have a say in matters on which he is not a specialist, he has to be an unusual one to be a success in his new environment. The second reason for caution about scientists being on the Boards or in top positions in Government concerns the extreme specialization of science, the result of which is that, apart from happy accidents, even scientists in different disciplines have great difficulty in communication. Some years ago, I remember A. L. Hodgkin, the Nobel Prize-winner in nerve physiology, and I going to a lecture given by the molecular biologist Sydney Brenner to a scientific Society at Cambridge. Neither of us felt that we knew much about molecular biology, so before the lecture I had a word with Brenner and said 'Look Sydney, Alan and I don't know a thing about molecular biology, nor will most of your audience. Will you therefore start at the beginning and treat us as if we were schoolboys?', which Brenner agreed to do. At the end of the lecture and the subsequent discussion, Hodgkin and I agreed we had not understood much of it. Yet Hodgkin, Brenner and I could all be described as biologists. How much less can a physicist be expected to know about molecular biology? I remember Blackett once saying, I thought rather peevishly, at a meeting of the Council for Scientific Policy: 'I wish someone could put down in one paragraph for me what molecular biology is.' These are examples of talk among scientists. You can imagine the difficulty a scientist has in having a working knowledge of ten different technical disciplines; nor is this problem going to be solved by radical changes in our educational system. One will still have to be a chemist to know what a sesquiterpenoid is, though if one is a scientist, one may be able to look it up in the index of a textbook of organic chemistry and thereafter have an extremely vague idea of the shape of the molecule.

I have been talking about very big organizations. It does, however, seem obvious that there is a stronger case for engineers being Directors of Engineering Companies; and for chemists to be Directors of Chemical Companies. But here again the engineer or chemist in question must have special qualities which not all engineers and scientists have. He will probably not develop these qualities unless he has experiences other than technical ones at a relatively early age. This raises a difficulty I have on several occasions noted in Shell. Like ICI, we have two ladders: one, a purely technical one and the other involving wider, managerial responsibilities. In one of our laboratories I spotted a very good scientist, aged about thirty-three, who I thought might have the right qualities for those wider, managerial, responsibilities. I talked to him about it and explained that if he wanted wider responsibilities, he would have to be tested in other parts of Shell. I told him I was pretty confident he would be successful. He told me he enjoyed his scientific work at the bench and did not want to give it up 'at any rate for the next five to ten years'. Wider managerial responsibilities, whether within research or on an even larger scale, cannot be developed too late in life, rarely after the age of forty. One must start at a receptive period of one's life and it is unfortunately the case that, in general, people become less receptive to new environments as they get older. If, therefore, someone is to become a research administrator or the Director of a large business or Government organization, he has got to be tested pretty early on in his career. Unfortunately, a two to three year absence from research is enough to make it very difficult to get back in if the test is unsuccessful.

At the beginning of this talk I said I was familiar with scientific language and the methods of research. This is something which every Research Director should be. He must know, in general terms, how scientists behave in laboratories and, I believe, be familiar with what might be called the basic English of science. What is that basic English? It would take too long to explain, but in the sixties and seventies, he will at least have to know that inertia does not mean laziness; that parabolic is not an old-fashioned medicine. He will certainly have to know what a control and a gene are. And that a fluidized bed is not something Christine Keeler had in her flat. Perhaps some Members of the Board should know about these things as well.

In an organization the size of Shell, I don't think there is any chance of an ex-research worker, by which I mean somebody who has had serious and successful research experience, being one of the six Managing Directors who, subject to the Boards, control the organization. There could, of course, be ex-research workers as part-time members of the Boards of Royal Dutch and Shell Transport & Trading; but I am not sure what they would do. You might counter what I have said by drawing attention to the fact that Professor Casimir, for example, a physicist with a world-wide reputation, is a Director of the giant Dutch electrical firm Philips. I don't know how many whole-time Directors Philips has, but I strongly suspect that a significant number of the Coordinators of the Royal Dutch-Shell Group would be classified as Directors if our organization were the same as that of Philips; and I expect that, in years to come, the Royal Dutch-Shell Group will evolve towards having more whole-time Directors though there will always be a small nucleus of Top Management, as I believe there is in Philips. Such Top Management might include people with a Ph.D., which implies three years of research, but not people such as Casimir with ten or fifteen years of research experience.

One of the things that strikes one very forcibly in industrial research is that a negligible amount is done without a clear-cut practical objective. We do not do research of the type 'We must learn all about the physiology of the cow' or 'We ought to research on micro-electronic circuitry' or 'We should research on ceramics'. Moreover, there is a clearly defined and accountable producer (of which research is only a part) and user of the end product. I have the impression, which perhaps some of you will be able to dispel, that this clearly-defined system of accountability and objectives does not always exist in Defence contracts. The user and the producer must not be asphyxiated by over-poweringly large staff groups; nor, once financial approval has been given for a project, should intermediate financial approvals be necessary from persons other than the user. Am I right in thinking that the simple structure I have tried to outline a few minutes ago does not exist in Government contracts and, if I am right, is there some good reason for the difference? It can't just be the size of the operations because when, in Shell, the decision was taken to buy more than twenty 200,000-ton tankers, extremely large sums of money were involved. But when the decision was taken, the Marine Coordinator got on with the job without continually having to refer back for financial approval and without the intervention of so-called Advisory Groups not of his own choosing. Of course, this implies that the Marine Coordinator was strictly accountable for the work and the producers of the tankers were accountable to him. If the first 200,000-ton tanker had broken in half or turned out to be uncontrollable, the Marine Coordinator would have had to carry the can.

Finally you may ask the question 'How do you know how much research the Royal Dutch-Shell Group should do?' The short answer is that I don't. Although, as mentioned earlier, the businessmen determine 89% of our research expenditure, in another, staff capacity, I have the duty of advising the Managing Directors and the Boards whether I think we are spending too much, too little, or about the right amount. Of course, in extreme cases, it would be easy to say we are spending too much because the expenditure would eat obviously and undesirably into Shell's profits. But this has not been the case for the last ten years. I am afraid that at present and, so far as I can see for an indefinite time to come, the answer to the question 'Are we doing enough, too little or the right amount of research?' will largely be based on intuition, and acceptance of the bill will, therefore, reflect the confidence that the Top Management have in their Research Director. All sorts of efforts have been made to be more objective and quantitative in such evaluations; but all the ones I have studied involve one unknown parameter which can be summed up by the statement 'Let's make a guess as to what would have happened if we had not spent that research money'. This is a dangerous premise on which to take action and not one which appeals to efficient companies. It is, of course, also possible to compare company X and company Y in regard to research expenditure, but such comparisons are difficult to make because different companies often express their research expenditure in very different ways. Moreover, there rarely are two very similar companies. So you arrive at the point that one must have a Research Director who, apart from knowing about research, must be cost-conscious and familiar with the business as it is at present and as it will be in ten years' time, when the current research will become commercial. And the bosses must have confidence in him. If they have not, machinery must exist to get rid of him in a reasonable way.

7

CONFLICT AND TENSION
IN INDUSTRIAL RESEARCH

Address to a Senior Shell Study Group
at Shell's Amsterdam Laboratory,
22 May 1968

ONE of the most senior and distinguished members of the Royal
Dutch-Shell Group engages each morning in an activity called
'jogging' in England. This might be described as stationary
running and, before or after his bath – I forget which – he does
400 jogs. This somewhat stresses his heart which he believes, no
doubt on the advice of Shell's Medical Function, is good for him
and keeps him fit. So stress or tension, properly rationed, may be
good for you and me.

It would be easy to give you what might be called a morale-
boosting talk and propagand you into believing that Shell's
research activities are excellent and so well integrated into the
business as to cause little anxiety. I do not say that such a talk,
which I have given to audiences less interested in and committed
to Shell than you, would be false or undesirable; but I do think
that, at the risk of being accused of washing in private some linen
which I am not prepared to designate as soiled, let alone dirty, it is
useful from time to time to record what, rightly or wrongly,
causes me conflict or tension, and what does the same, in regard
to research, to other Shell research workers and those with whom
they are in contact in Shell. Of course, what worries me may not
have worried my predecessors and may well not worry my
successors. Some of these worries, however, are virtually in-
escapable in any industrial research organization.

I referred to Shell's research workers being in contact with
other members of Shell, sometimes called the businessmen. Some
five years ago a Managing Director said to me 'You know that in
the past our research was rather a sacred cow. All that is going to
change from now on', to which I made some inarticulate
mumblings in reply. In fact parts of our research have continued

to be what some people might call a sacred cow and will continue to be so in the future, in a particular sense, which was well summed up by a previous Group Research Coordinator who said:

'One of the complicating elements is the fact that one is dealing with highly trained and specialized individuals, hard to find and much in demand, who are sensitive to the environment in which they work. No research laboratory could long exist if there were repeated and frequent changes in the size of its professional staff. Both increases and decreases must be undertaken with caution and with a long-range policy in mind.'

I do not say this statement asserts that research is more of a sacred cow than, for example, Shell's Legal Division in The Hague; nor do I believe that scientists should be treated as priests, high, medium or low; nor do I see why our research workers should be more sensitive to their environment than anyone else in Shell. Whoever has worked in Shell Centre in London and has suffered from the air-conditioning system, with those periodic puffs of vanilla ice cream, will certainly have something to say about the environment in which he works and his sensitivity to it. Nevertheless, quite a few of Shell's activities, including research, are sacred cows in that one cannot change the size or direction of effort at short notice, nor without very serious consideration of the future consequences of such action. Without wishing to appear parochial, I do believe this emphatically applies to the Research Function. One must be very careful indeed before engaging in a course of action which, among other disadvantages, might upset members of our laboratories. At the very least this will impair their efficiency and usefulness to Shell; at the worst, by the wrong treatment, one may lose a man whom it is difficult, if not impossible, to replace, again with serious consequences for Shell. I know of a number of such key people here in Holland, in America and in England.

Looking back over the ten or so years since I have been in Shell, I am sometimes not sure if we *have* proceeded with caution in research. We have shut one laboratory in the United Kingdom, one in Germany and one in the USA. During the same period we have set up two new laboratories in the United Kingdom and greatly expanded the size of a third. These changes imply quite a formidable series of upheavals in research and I do not believe we can continue in this way even if we want to, which we don't. The point is that if one closes two laboratories and establishes two others, the net effect is not zero. It adds up to four upheavals. Both the closure and the establishment of laboratories put a great strain on those concerned with the operation and with the integration of the new system into Shell. Yet we are faced with a rate of expenditure increase, at any rate on this side of the Atlantic, which disturbs me, even though our numbers remain pretty well constant and we believe that the output per laboratory man is going up. In other words, this increase in expenditure is caused by factors which we normally describe as being 'outside our control'. But are they? When in the Netherlands or the United Kingdom we have an across-the-board salary increase, should we counterbalance its cost by an appropriate reduction in manpower? Are our laboratories stretched to the limit in the sense that the businessmen who control 89% of our laboratory programmes and budgets will see their segments of the business suffer as a result of such contractions? Or do those of us who also have the duty of looking further ahead see difficulties arising out of such action, N years hence, where N may, perhaps, lie between ten and twenty years? Would inter-company co-operative research in certain areas, where exclusivity is of secondary importance, help to reduce the bill? Should we arbitrarily fix an annual rate of expenditure increase of not more than 6%, which somehow or other, for totally illogical reasons, seems to me orderly, provided we don't have to increase our manpower? Is it really worth trying to compare our research activity with that of Standard Oil of New Jersey, incidentally the only company with which Shell's research as a whole is worth comparison? And if we found we were spending more or had more research workers than Jersey, so what? Is there any reason why Jersey should be right and Shell wrong? It is no good comparing earning powers because, as we all know, our situations are very different.

I have been describing a particular tension and conflict to which the senior research management is subjected, whether in a particular laboratory or in the Central Offices, in having to look in two different directions at the same time. One is the direction of the businessmen and top management of the Group; the other is towards the research workers themselves, with the knowledge that in the sixties and seventies, because of the shortage of good scientists, engineers and mathematicians, many, if not most, of our most valuable research workers can rather easily get jobs elsewhere, and sometimes under better conditions than we can or do provide.

There has not been much tendency for our research workers to leave Shell once they are over a comparatively short incubation period; but I am not sure this will go on and I am not even sure that it should go on. I would like to see more short-term, that is five-year, interchanges between the members of our laboratories and other organizations, whether industrial, academic or Government. I know the difficulties, but nevertheless I believe it a useful concept to foster.

So one has to do a tight-rope act, balancing the desires and aspirations of the research workers, which vary from wanting to climb up the ladder, publishing a paper in a learned journal, or making a patentable discovery, against the wishes of the Managing Directors and Boards whose actions are properly in the interests of the shareholders. Such a balancing act, which may induce both tension and conflict, also includes what might roughly be called acting, or the development of a schizophrenic personality. It would not be right and of questionable value to talk to Kloosterziel at our Amsterdam Laboratory or Cornforth at Milstead Laboratory in the same way as one talks to Managing Director Starrenburg and his colleagues. The difference may involve acting, to one or the other audience, as does the following situation: what may seem to be fundamental research to a man at the bench may obviously be applied research in my book. Yet sometimes it may be unwise to labour the latter point.

Another piece of acting, or is a better word dissimulation, concerns the phenomenon called Highlights. Once a year I present to the Boards of Royal Dutch and Shell Transport & Trading an Annual Report, in which there is a section called Highlights, which contains a list of some twenty-five discoveries our laboratories made during the previous year. While many of the items are interesting, if somewhat incomprehensible to the lay members of the Boards who constitute the majority, I believe that Highlights give a false picture of our research activities. Our senior Managing Director Brouwer put it neatly when, in a recent article, he described our research as Shell's 'technical conscience'. Much of our activity is not designed to produce highlights, but is an essential and inevitable concomitant of the operations of a vast industrial enterprise. Brouwer agrees with my view that we should stop producing these Highlights, but I do not know how the Boards will react to not being titillated. If we make one major money-making breakthrough every ten years – such as the Rijswijk Laboratory's sand consolidation process or something equally important – we shall be doing pretty well; and we shall be lucky if the breakthrough occurs, for example, in the sixth year of the ten year period. When it occurs, it should of course be highlighted to the Boards and, indeed, across the board.

In the old days, if I understand the situation correctly, the businessmen did not have so much say about what our laboratories did and how much they cost, as they do today. There was an occasion, I think in the autumn of 1961, when the Managing Directors got fed up and said 'you cannot have as much money in 1962'; but since then our research has been functionalized, which means that the businessmen sponsor 89% of our research expenditure, the other 11% being General Research. This in turn brings tension and conflict because not all of our Functions are equally sophisticated in regard to research. Nor do all of them contain experienced research administrators. Some Functions are satisfied with a constant effort and will 'ride with inflation'. How long O Lord, one might ask. Others want an annual 1% decrease in effort. Another would like an increased research effort on a problem which I suspect is intractable if not insoluble. Some are rather allergic to research. The Group Research Co-ordinator has, roughly, two duties: one is to provide an efficient research service; the other is a staff duty, to advise the Managing Directors and Boards whether we are doing too much research, too little or, hopefully, about the right amount. This activity, which might be likened to looking into an opaque crystal ball in the dark, causes me considerable stress and, at times, conflict, both with the laboratories and with the businessmen. And let me say, I hope for the last time, that there is no general method of quantitatively assessing the profitability of research even though some quite complicated mathematical papers have been written on the subject. In other words, this and some other aspects of research administration are to a considerable extent an art at which some people are extremely good, like Fiske and Pierce of Bell Telephones, even though, for certain technical reasons, they are in a somewhat privileged position.

Even if we, the Research Function, are convinced that we are doing the right amount of research for each Function, and on the right subjects, we cannot and should not be complacent. Information churned out by the Research Function must be turned into technical progress if it is to be of use to the business. The value of information which is not so used is rapidly discounted. It is, of course, the responsibility of the Function concerned quickly and properly to use information we give them; but this can only be done effectively if the Function and Research have a real understanding of each other's jobs and difficulties. There is, therefore, a problem of information flow in integrating research into Shell's business. I don't have to tell you that communication failures are almost in a class by themselves as a cause of conflict and tension.

A further cause of conflict and tension in Shell's research concerns nationalism, both on the part of people and their Governments. I once asked Starrenburg whether he felt nationalistic, to which he replied 'No, except when I should', a characteristic and good answer. Of course there are from time to time inter-national problems between people in research. Some people, by virtue of upbringing and environment, are less international in outlook than others. But the main headache is Governmental nationalism. 'Why', a Government may say, 'should we in country X be dependent on country Y for our technological know-how, and, moreover, have to pay for it in foreign currency? Why can't we do the research ourselves? Indeed, we intend to do it and to stop being dependent on those outsiders.' As members of this Group have particularly good reasons to know because you come from different countries, this problem affects Shell in France, Canada and Italy; and, probably, Australia and Japan in the fairly near future. Whether it will affect us in Germany or not is an open question. It does not affect us in the Netherlands and the UK provided there is what might be called a reasonable balance of glamour between the two countries, which I think we have at the moment. This is a serious problem, both from the point of view of the countries concerned and of Shell, because if we have to start research, for example, in Italy or Australia, it will either put the bill up above its present level of £50 million* a year, or we must reduce research in the Netherlands or the UK, which would not be in our interests.

Many people say that for historical reasons (that hackneyed phrase), Shell has too many laboratories. Depending on the definition of a laboratory, we have about twenty-six. Would it be a good thing to have less? Are very large laboratories more efficient and economical than smaller ones? I am inclined to think that a laboratory with about 700 people in it is best. Jan Choufoer, the Director of our Amsterdam Laboratory, in which there are 2000 people, thinks differently, I believe; but the Bell Telephone Laboratories have recently been split up. Is it reasonable for what I might call refinery R & D to be done by Shell at a large laboratory in California, at a large laboratory in Texas and at a large laboratory at Amsterdam? Does Jersey do this? Is it worth asking the question, given that these laboratories exist and that the possibility of terminating the activity in one of them is in the neighbourhood of zero? I do not myself think that having a mass of laboratories, difficult as it may be to remember what each of them does except in very general terms, is necessarily a disadvantage. I do think that very small laboratories, such as Milstead in England and the Shell Pipeline Corporation Laboratory at Houston, even if they have got the minimum quantum of research effort to make their work in particular fields successful, suffer from a lack of manpower flexibility. It would be impossible, for example, to reduce their numbers to keep the annual expenditure increase down to some predetermined level, a course of action whose desirability I questioned earlier. Why not join small laboratories up with other neighbouring ones? During a particular block of time it may be impossible to fuse laboratories, even when they are literally next door to each other. This applies, for example, in the case of the Central Laboratories at Egham and Egham Industrial Chemicals Laboratory. There would be some advantages in there just being the Egham Laboratory, but at the moment it is administratively impossible to achieve this.

* £105 million in 1975, at £1 = $2.02.

I do not know whether, in this talk, you will think I justified the title. Of course I think I have, even if the conflicts and tensions arising out of the subjects I have been discussing were somewhat camouflaged. Let me end with a quotation, which you may find rather anarchical, by Dr Mees, the Vice-President (Research) of the Eastman Kodak Company in the USA. Perhaps it cuts down to size those like me, who are paid to think about the things – and a few others – which were the subject of my talk to you this afternoon. Dr Mees said:

'The best person to decide what research work shall be done is the man who is doing the research, and the next best person is the head of the department, who knows all about the subject and the work; after that you leave the field of the best people and start on increasingly worse groups, the first being the research director, who is probably wrong more than half the time; and then a committee, which is wrong most of the time; and finally, a committee of vice-presidents of the company, which is wrong all the time.'

8

PURE AND APPLIED
RESEARCH

The Trueman Wood Lecture to the Royal Society of Arts,
8 December 1971[9]

The genesis of this and the next lecture was a report *The Organization and Management of Government R. & D.* which appeared in November 1971 under my name in a Government Green Paper (Command 4814) entitled *A Framework for Government Research & Development.* My report evoked squeals of anger, Gadarene-like in their intensity, from the scientific establishment. No less than 121 scientists and/or doctors signed letters of protest to *The Times.* What was the cause of the uproar? I believe it to have been as follows:

(i) I recommended that part of the money the Research Councils received from the Department of Education and Science should come instead from the appropriate Ministry, for example the Ministry of Agriculture, Fisheries and Food in the case of the Agricultural Research Council.

(ii) That when a Department supported a Research Council, that support should be on a customer-contractor basis. The phrase 'customer-contractor' was resented by many scientists – though a number understood and accepted the concept but were frightened to say so in public. Further references to this phrase will be found in this and the following chapter.

(iii) The report was terse. Exception was taken to this in general, and in particular to the phrase 'the customer says what he wants; the contractor does it (if he can); and the customer pays'.

The report contained fifty-five recommendations and I have no idea how many of them have been implemented. One of the recommendations was that the Chief Scientific Adviser to the Government should be charged with monitoring the implementation (or non-implementation, I suppose) of the recommendations.

Much of the fuss which followed the report concerned semantic questions, for example the exact meaning of such phrases as tactical research, strategic research, pure research and a large number of others, which I have attempted to analyse and define in an article in *Nature* called *45 Varieties of Research.*[10]

There was an important omission in the *published* version of my report which, if only for professional reasons, should be rectified. No scientist would have the temerity or stupidity to recommend the transfer of large sums of money from one Department to another without assigning tolerances to the recommended figures. A tolerance of plus or minus 15% should be assigned to all the transfers I recommended. It is important to emphasize that 'plus or minus' means precisely what it says. It has nothing to do with the statistician's Standard Error or Standard Deviation. I greatly deprecate this omission though it was not picked up, at any rate in public.

*

WHEN I was a scientist I was often frustrated and sometimes irritated by not knowing what the animals were to which my scientific colleagues referred, in Latin, in their learned papers: not only what those animals were, but where they fitted into the animal kingdom. Was *Asconema* a worm, a sponge, or even, perhaps, a plant? Could they not give the English as opposed to the Latin name? But here I found a difficulty. The robin is a quite different bird in America from what it is here and, by the same token, the rabbit is not a rabbit. In my own sphere of work, I found that the animal in which I was interested and whose ovaries you may sometimes have eaten when holidaying in the Mediterranean, was sometimes called a sea hedgehog, sometimes an egg urchin, or a sea egg, or an egg fish, a button-fish, a needle shell, a chestnut, a burr, a spike, a zart, a sea borer, a porcupine and, from time to time, a whore's egg. So the English names of animals are not of much help to know what they are; and I decided to learn the hard way, which was to write a simple book on the classification of living animals; and I soon realized that the intention was easier than the implementation. Not only are taxonomists the most violent, if not virulent, critics of each other; but also there seemed, as always, to be no absolute truth. Were animals really animals? Were there not so many borderline cases as to make distinctions rather questionable? Worse still, though it did not affect me at that time, was it obvious what was alive and what was not?

I laboured on, with shoulders preternaturally bent by such awesome responsibilities, irritating a number of people, but enjoying the task – I mean, of course, the work, not irritating people. The end product was, without undue modesty, of little value; and it was sharply criticized for its inadequacies by at least one pundit, whom, incidentally, I had consulted beforehand and whose advice I had taken. But classification is necessary, if only because the 5000 or so animals mentioned in the index of my book have little or no meaning or use until they can be fitted into a structure, skeleton or matrix which has a logical and biological *raison d'être*.

So it is with science and research; and research workers, particularly ex-research workers who are the high priests of the cult, have not been inhibited in getting on to the taxonomic bandwaggon, nor from criticizing the classification of others. In the Zuckerman report issued by Her Majesty's Stationery Office in 1961,[11] one finds it is convenient, which some people might say is Civil Service-ese for mandatory, to classify research into the following categories. First, there is 'pure basic research', said to be carried out solely to increase scientific knowledge: that is knowledge of the nature of the material world. Can we not research on the nature of the immaterial world, the world of thought, religion, ethics and morality? And if we can, is that impure basic research, or pure non-basic research, or pure basic non-research, because it is immaterial? One had better ask Zuckerman.

Pure basic research was said to be identical with 'fundamental', 'pure' or 'basic' research. So when, later, I use the adjective basic, you will know that I could equally well have said fundamental or pure.

Then, according to Zuckerman, there is 'objective basic research', which denotes basic research in fields of 'recognized potential technological importance'. It has the quality of relevance to some definable technological objective. An example might be of the study of the turbulent flow of liquids, which is quite important for ships, torpedoes and pipelines. If our knowledge of turbulence and the mathematics associated with it is inadequate for the technological objective in view, we engage or indulge in objective basic research.

Then there is 'applied project research', which has as its objective some practical goal. Some of us might just call it applied research.

After that comes 'applied operational research', which seems to be concerned with improving things which already exist. The phrase is unfortunate because operational research, like the robin, has two quite different meanings.

Finally, there is 'development', which is said to bridge the gap between research and production. It may involve the design and operation of pilot plants and, according to accounting procedures, prototypes.

So much for Zuckerman, and one wonders for whom this elaborate taxonomy was necessary and to whom it is useful.

Others, needless to say, have had different ideas and have divided the package into basic research with its usual meaning; 'strategic research', which I believe to mean research in a field of possible application but without any specific objective; and, finally, 'tactical research', which I think means research which has a practical objective as its end product. This also is unfortunate because the phrase tactical research may give the impression of short-term study, whereas one may have to work for many years to achieve a practical objective. It took Dr Sternbach of Hoffman La-Roche some twenty-five years to discover the tranquillizers Librium, Valium and Mogadon, but the advantage of having achieved the practical objective of his researches are obvious.

Faced by these semantic acrobatics and complexities, I reverted to my animals and their reproduction which interested me at the time; and I realized what was wrong: that these classifications, which, we must assume, have some value judging by the eminence of their originators, at best implied diving in at the deep end before having a paddle in less dangerous waters. At worst they raised the possibility of drowning in a sea of taxonomy. So, in case some of you, like me, are not terribly strong swimmers, let us start at the shallow end and see where we get, even if, in due course, the water becomes deep and, from time to time, rather murky. In the shallow end there are only two sorts of research; one is called basic and the other applied.

Basic research is done solely to increase knowledge. It is, practically speaking, 'useless'. It is often motivated by the curiosity of an individual, whether he be the person who does the research or that person's boss.

There are some important ground rules for the basic research worker, apart from the obvious ones of knowing how to set about the job and being good at it. He must never try to justify his activities on the grounds that they may help mankind. He must not, therefore, remind us of those rare cases when this has happened – of Rutherford, who some people claim to have been the father of the atomic bomb, if that was such a great help to mankind; and of nuclear power, which may well save mankind, when fossil fuels run out, as they certainly will; nor must he remind us of Fleming, whose powers of observation, so typical of the top-class scientist, were responsible for the discovery of penicillin. The pure research worker doesn't have to bail himself out with these excuses. Society tolerates and encourages him or her, albeit with a little more reserve than ten to twenty years ago when the sacerdotalism of science was at its zenith. We, society, shall go on backing good people and letting them do more or less what they want, provided what they want is not too obviously anti-social. Whether society will go on backing *every* Tom, Dick and Harry who is inquisitive but not too gifted, and let them do what they like at public expense for three or so years at a university after graduation, is a matter on which we would do well to ponder. We do not want to have too many lift attendants, taxi-drivers or uniformed commissionaires with Ph.D.s in the Natural Sciences; and if we don't watch out, we may be in danger of meeting one of these when we decide on an evening's pleasure seeing *The Devils*, if it is still on.

If he or she is good – and, in spite of the occasional clanger, I think we have reasonable yardsticks to make the measurements to justify such an assertion – we must let them go on, even if, to some of us, the things about which they are inquisitive seem remote, strange, incomprehensible, out of this world and, indeed, out of all other worlds, for that matter. I quote, with some explanatory interpolations, from a recent number of the *New Scientist and Science Journal*: 'Professor Wheeler, a cosmologist of world distinction, describes his field of study as the chemistry of geometry in superspace, where neither time nor space exist, but which is the true reality.' What is the good of Professor Wheeler's studies, some of you may ask? 'What is the good of a new-born baby?' Faraday said to Queen Victoria, in answer to a similar question. Or perhaps it was Benjamin Franklin. Nobody is sure.

So much for basic research and the discoveries of practical importance which occasionally are, but almost always are not, made, accidentally, during its prosecution. I do not denigrate nor under-rate them; but I assert that the needs of our country are too important, urgent and identifiable to rely on chance discoveries – to warrant those needs being left to a form of scientific roulette in which there are many more numbers for the ball to enter than the conventional thirty-seven.

I come now to the second sort of research, called applied research or, as I prefer, applied research and development. It is indistinguishable from pure research as regards *how* it is done. The distinction lies in *why* it is done and *who* wants it done. Its tempo may also be somewhat less leisurely than that of the work of people such as myself who remained for the scientifically important years of my life in that delightful and stimulating ivory tower called Cambridge University.

Somebody wants some applied research done, not because he wants the applied research but because he deems it necessary to achieve an objective, which also needs for its fulfilment the interplay of disciplines and expertise other than research. What is that objective? The answer is a rather Cantorian one: there are as many objectives which require applied research as there are subjects which stimulate the attention of the basic research worker.

We may wish to put a living man on the moon for childish, geological or military reasons, or a mixture of all three. We may wish to provide the blind with artificial eyes that enable them to see – and this is not just a silly, unrealizable pipe-dream. We may wish that cars in this city would make less noise and emit less exhaust gases. We may wish to stop or reduce the number of collisions between ships in the English Channel, or near-misses over London Airport. We may wish to have three-dimensional colour television screens which could make sight-seeing and travel less important than they are today. Why should I go to the bother and expense of visiting Niagara Falls if I can see it, looking, perhaps, even better than the original, in my home at Cambridge? What else would you like? You may well be able to have it. As A. C. Clarke said, anything that can be done will be done. But is this true? Even if he has been right so far, will he be right in the future? Much as I admire A. C. Clarke and his predictive genius, I do not believe that from now on, whatever may have happened before, anything that can be done will be done. We have, in fact, got to the end of the road. From now on the man who determines the objective for which applied research is necessary has got to justify the objective to a form of shareholder, whether it be the electorate and their representatives in Parliament, or that somewhat elusive and inarticulate person, the shareholder in a company.

So, for ultimately the same reasons, there is from now on going to be more careful scrutiny of basic *and* applied research. In the case of the former, it will not necessarily be the objective which will be under scrutiny, but the abilities and qualities of the research worker who wishes to spend quite a while – and the nation's resources – studying superspace and reality. But it is not difficult to foresee that certain forms of basic research, motivated by the intrinsic interest of the subject, might have dangerous consequences or side-effects; and that society will not readily acquiesce in such research being pursued and to the results being disseminated in a completely indiscriminate, uncontrolled and, on occasions, irresponsible way. Just as we do not allow the indiscriminate use of persistent insecticides in this country, sooner or later we shall have to control those types of basic research whose indiscriminate exploitation would or might be harmful to society. Interference with the liberty of the subject? Yes, but is there ever, in reality, absolute liberty? I think not.

There is another 'if' or 'but' about basic research, which applies only to what is nowadays called the 'Big' variety. In a recent issue of *The Economist* there was an enjoyable article entitled 'Protons on the Prairie' in which one learns that some 6800 acres of cornfields near Chicago have been turned into 'the world's largest instrument for basic research', for which Congress authorized the expenditure of a mere $250 million, or about £100 million. This instrument, will, needless to say, be used to search for new particles, described in the article as 'the building blocks of nature'. With it, scientists will, doubtless, discover that some structureless, fundamental particles are not really like that at all; and that in reality, if I dare use that word, they are like onions whose further dissection will need a new instrument costing not

£100 million but £1000 or £10,000 million. But that is not all: Mr Downs, the chief architect of the Proton Prairie, has a 'strong programme to provide jobs for minority groups and to make the laboratory's pleasant rolling prairie land an area of natural beauty'. An employment office has been set up in Chicago to recruit black workers; three artificial lakes have been made for fishermen; and, needless to say, Mr Wilson, in charge of the project, has brought to the Proton Prairie two herds of buffalo.

We cannot afford a gadget costing so much as this in the United Kingdom, with or without the lakes and buffaloes; but in our own modest way, we have similar intentions. The scientific establishment has announced how essential it is for the nation (and, parenthetically, for its scientific welfare), to build a High Flux Beam Reactor, whatever that is. Without it, needless to say, we shall lag behind the rest of the scientific world. Even that sacred subject, molecular biology, will be illuminated by this instrument. Obviously, it is not the job of the scientific establishment to advise, though they might ponder, on whether the money this instrument will cost could be better spent on other things, for example:

Titian's *Death of Actaeon* (less than 10%)
20 miles of motorway
4 hospitals
300 Adventure Playgrounds for underprivileged children
Three 1000-inmate prisons
200,000 television sets for the old and housebound
2 Jumbo jets
4500 houses.

This study of Opportunity Costs, as the professionals choose to describe resource allocation, is one of the central, if not the central, problems of our times; and it is clear that basic science, and big science in particular, cannot be exceptional and absolved from being put under the Opportunity Cost microscope.

In applied research the quality and creativity of the worker are no less important and will influence, if not determine, whether the programme is done or not; but in addition, something else, a different factor, comes into consideration. Do we approve of the objective, not only morally, but also economically? Can we afford it? Is there a pay-off for our country? Pay-off in the sense,

75

for example, that the countryside is cleaner, that the air is purer, that our balance of payments is better, that law and order will be maintained more efficiently, that taxation will be reduced, if that is credible. You can add to the list yourselves indefinitely.

It seems obvious that these deep and fundamental national questions cannot be decided by scientists alone and it is here that I believe this country, like some others, is somewhat anachronistic. Please do not be alarmed, I am not about to recommend a totalitarian, *dirigiste* regime in which our scientists will be indistinguishable from rats on their perpetually revolving scientific treadmills. We all know that such direction or coercion would be counter-productive. But if we are anachronistic, how are we anachronistic and what should be done about it?

The anachronism to which I refer can be summed up by the phrase Pedestalization of Science, particularly in respect of applied research by virtue of the admiration, indeed reverence, we have for pure science. Have we not got 4.6 Nobel Prize-winners per ten million of our people, in comparison with America's 3.3? There may have been a time when scientists knew what was best for their country and, therefore, with almost equal illogicality, what ought to be done. I say with almost equal illogicality because there is no *a priori* reason why someone with scientific training *should* know best what ought to be done; and also because even if he did, there is just as little reason why he should know how to do it. Scientists, of course, have their role to play in the study of such problems as urban conglomerations, the information explosion, absenteeism, the quality of life (if one can define it), the agricultural needs of the country, road safety and drug addiction; but the scientist only has a role in the attack on these non-Wheeleresque problems, just as do sociologists, engineers, lawyers, economists, accountants, mathematicians and administrators, not to speak of our rulers, the politicians. But this is not quite how things work out. One still finds, to a certain extent in industry, and in Government, that the old philosophy 'Spot good scientists, get them, and let them get on with the job', though inadequate and anachronistic, still plays too important a role in determining the objectives, the applied research and, unfortunately from time to time, the development these objectives require, both in this and other countries. It is not wholly the fault of the scientists that this outmoded credo has persisted, though they have not been slow to invoke the equally outmoded Haldane Principle to justify scientific freedom, independence, or indeed, *laissez-faire*, both within and outside Government, and in applied as in pure research. But few of those who invoke this so-called Principle have, in fact, bothered to read what the old boy, or rather his Committee, said, more than fifty years ago. The specific scientific policies mentioned by the Committee were designed:

to promote an increase of material production;
to promote the health of the entire community; and
to apply science to industry.

Few would question the inadequacy of these policies for the seventies; and it is hard to put the clock back a mere fifty years and visualize a society in which such diffuse precepts could have had much meaning or achieved any useful results. This is not to say that they had no effect, some of them good. On the contrary, the effects are still with us: one of these is the polarization of society into scientists, and to a lesser extent, technologists – and the rest. Not only has this adversely affected Government research and development, Department by Department; but it also catalyzed the emergence of autonomous bodies, the Research Councils, accountable to Parliament as all Government agencies directly or indirectly must be, but not accountable to anyone else, in spite of their names, which include such bizarre words as 'agricultural', 'medical' and 'natural environment'. Is it not strange that though the taxpayer pays for these bodies, he has no say in what they do? 'Not a bit', the scientist replies:

'Who is the taxpayers' representative anyway?'

'Do you really not understand that scientists can't just be told to cure cancer or coronaries?'

'Did you really not know that we have Assessors, representing Government Departments, on our Councils? It is true that, in theory, they may not speak unless asked to do so, and they cannot vote; but they are influential and important people.'

'Have you not heard that research can't proceed in straight

lines and that it often *has* to go off course, even to the extent of making U-turns?'

'Do you really want to try and force good scientists to do work which doesn't appeal to them? Don't you see that this will harm the quality of the work, even if it is done at all in such circumstances?'

'Do you not know that we are constantly in touch with farmers, doctors, environmentalists, industrialists, civil servants and, indeed, all those to whose advice we can usefully listen (though we don't have to take it)?'

And, sometimes, a slug of the old gobbledygook:

'Science is indivisible; it is inter-disciplinary and lateral.'

'Finally, if by some remote chance, you are sufficiently demented to suggest there should be some formal relationship between us and Government Departments who might think they were concerned with our affairs, has it escaped your notice that politicians are dominated by considerations of power, constituencies and pressure groups; and that they are supported by faceless bureaucrats who, more often than not, are positively hostile towards us and our work, because they can't understand it?'

I said a little while ago that scientists were not wholly responsible for the 'let them get on with the job' philosophy; and, indeed, it would be surprising if they were; because we scientists are neither black, selfish, thoughtless and unpatriotic; nor are we white, selfless and thoughtful patriots. Like virtually everyone else we are grey curate's eggs. And like everyone else, we are just a teeny bit resistant to change, particularly if we are not 100% certain that the change will be for the better. Better the devil you know etc., but the trouble lies in the devil, for which I do believe Haldane and his Committee must take a good deal of responsibility. The devil to which I refer and which I have already mentioned is the polarization of activities, particularly in Government, into those that are scientific, or even 'technical'; and those that are not. This polarization has resulted in there being almost no interchange of people between the Civil Service as we know it, and the Scientific Civil Service and analogous bodies. Do not be misled into believing this is due to administrative, financial or geographical difficulties. Those, if and when they exist, are secondary. The block is caused by the belief, on the one hand, that an administrator cannot possibly have an important role to play in a scientific or technological community; and, on the other hand, that scientists are, almost by definition, bad administrators and will therefore need a lot of training to do anything but science and, even then, will probably be no good. Neither proposition is true, needless to say – that grey egg is the answer again.

It will, I think, be clear that I believe something is wrong. 'What do you suggest should be done about it?' you might ask. Curiously enough I am not too worried about the last worry I mentioned – the lack of movement into and out of the Scientific Civil Service. I believe this problem will be solved during the next five or so years, particularly if we study the ways in which some industries cope with it. What worries me most is the conduct of the activity in which applied research and development is involved. From 13 to 17% of the Government's research expenditure is on basic research and I have few worries about it, apart from its cost and in spite of some pitfalls I can see ahead and which I have mentioned. Basic research is an activity in its own right, but applied research and development is not – that is why I used the cumbersome phrase 'activity in which applied research and development is involved'. Applied research is one of the human activities which may be necessary to achieve a practical objective. The research worker should *not* formulate the objective, though he can and should help. The research worker should *not* decide that the objective requires research for its achievement. He should *not* decide that the research should be done, assuming it is necessary. He should *not* decide when to stop. Nor should he decide to change the objective in mid-stream, however desirable it may seem to him to do so. What then remains for the research worker to do? The answer is an enjoyable one for him and quite simple, even if the execution is difficult: do the research and help that other man, who has the onerous task of doing all those things you are not to do, as much as you can. He will need all the help he can get, if only because his responsibilities may be both new and strange to him – this is the worrying thing. Even the formulation of an objective is a complex and difficult undertaking, one of the hardest parts of which is to avoid the inclusion, in the formulation, of hidden assumptions. They may seem almost obvious, but the great mathematician, G. H. Hardy, had this to say about this phrase:[12]

'When one says that something is 'almost obvious' one may mean one or other of two things. One may mean 'it is difficult to doubt the truth of the statement', or 'the statement is such as common sense instinctively accepts', as it accepts, for example, the truth of the proposition $2+2=4$. That a statement is 'obvious' in this sense does not prove that it is true, since the most confident of the intuitive judgements of common sense are often found to be mistaken.'

So much for one meaning of the almost obvious. Let us now examine, in a little detail, a particular objective which the customer for applied research and development might formulate: *make an electric car.* Our customer clearly believes that the electric car has advantage over the conventional, internal combustion variety. What are these advantages?

First, the electric car is quieter, not being dependent on a continuous series of explosions for its propulsion.

Secondly, the electric car is cleaner – it produces no exhaust gases or soot.

Thirdly, it would make us less dependent on oil from unpredictable, or too easily predictable, parts of the world.

Fourthly – and this requires a rather sophisticated, if misguided customer – electric cars are more efficient than petrol-driven ones, because they are not limited by the physical laws that govern heat engines.

None of these four, obvious advantages are necessarily true. Some electric cars are not quieter than petrol-driven ones, because of the noise made by their ancillary equipment such as fans, pumps and motors. Electric cars *may* produce exhaust gases. Whether they are driven by fuel cells or batteries, they will not necessarily make us independent of imported oil. The fourth reason, though often cited, is just wrong, for technical reasons with which I need not weary you.

But there are other difficulties which the customer must take into consideration before formulating the objective 'make an electric car'. It may take quite a while, ten to twenty years, to achieve. Shall we want cars then? Or will there be automatic, publicly-owned and mains-operated capsules? If we do have battery-operated electric cars, how will they be recharged? Will filling stations become battery stores with recharging facilities? Won't that need a lot of rewiring throughout the country? And, by the way, shall we have enough electrical generating capacity in the country to cope with the new demand? By the way again, can one make an electric car with a reasonable performance? What is reasonable?

When these questions – and a good few more – have been answered or partly answered, the customer is in a position to start talking to the applied research worker, if he has been so stupid as not to do so earlier. Then the customer may get his first of many shocks, because the applied research worker may say 'There is no hope of achieving your objective unless you first agree to fifty man-years of basic electrochemical research. Sorry, but we just don't know enough about how different electric batteries perform and work'.

I hope I have said enough to show that the customer who formulates or defines the objective which needs research and development for its fulfilment has, as I said earlier, an onerous task, even at the very beginning; and he will need all the help he can get from economists, sociologists, environmentalists *and* scientists. Why bother to make this distinction between the customer and his contractor for R & D? Why not leave such matters to the research workers themselves? The answer, apart from the true but unsatisfying one 'Daddy knows best', is that research workers soon lose their research skills when they leave their laboratories. But if they do, let us hope that some, at any rate, will sever the umbilical cords to their laboratories and become customers.

During this lecture, I have tried to make the case for greater control, on what, for short, can be called a customer-contractor basis, of research and development, apart from basic research. I don't much care whether the basic research is of what I call the Wheeleresque variety, or whether it is basic research in the field of medicine, agriculture or industry, though it is not only the practising scientist, but also the customer, who will call for this latter type of basic research when he sees the gaps in scientific knowledge which hinder the achievement of the objective he has in mind. What, however, I do object to is virtually all medical, agricultural and environmental research being controlled, autonomously, by scientists and, to a lesser extent, engineers and mathematicians, with concomitant downgrading of the research commissioned by Government Departments and, with a few exceptions such as the Bell Telephone Laboratories, by Industry. We must, I believe, oppose the deliberate creation and nurture of this kind of scientific élite – the autonomous have's and the departmental or industrial have not's. But it would be quite wrong of me not to mention that my philosophy is anathema to very many scientists, particularly, of course, to some of those intimately connected with our Research Council system. And they have conferred the beatification of the scientific establishment on Haldane and his acolyte, the late Lord Addison, for their efforts in preserving the autonomy and lack of functional accountability of the Research Councils. Sir Harold Himsworth, Secretary of the Medical Research Council for nineteen years, had this to say about the horrors and iniquities, if not disasters, that would have occurred if Addison, as he says twice in one paragraph, had 'failed':[13]

> 'Parliament and country would thereby have been deprived of access to a permanent source of informed opinion on matters of acute political concern, such as the hazards of "fall-out" from atomic explosions, the safety of new vaccines, the rationing of food in war time, the risks of economically important habits like cigarette smoking and the dangers of particular industrial operations, which by its independence of the interests involved, could be generally accepted as disinterested and unselected.'

You will, I am sure, have noticed serious fallacies in this declaration of faith, so I will only mention three; first, do we accept that scientists are so corrupt and contemptible as deliberately to select their results and stop being disinterested when they do not work for, or in, an autonomous organization? Secondly, can anyone believe that a Minister of the Crown and his Permanent Secretary can, in the seventies, afford or, even, be able to suppress the facts about the hazards of 'fall-out' or smoking? Thirdly, the author seems to have forgotten that the medical subjects he mentions are not the exclusive property of the United Kingdom. Many other nations research on them and will publish the results, with devastating effects on our politicians if they have been so venal as to suppress the results of the same work done in this country.

It really won't work. The sacerdotalism of science is no longer at its zenith.

Taken or quoted out of context some of the observations I have made in this lecture could be construed to imply that I am anti-science and anti-scientists. It should be unnecessary for me to say the reverse is the case; but I do think the scientific community must be careful not to cling, inordinately long, to outdated concepts. As always, the transition, or perhaps I should say step function, is difficult to take. But I am sure it is essential.

Michael Shanks recently wrote an article in *The Times* called 'The Who, Why and What of Science Policy'. There may have to be a policy for basic science, if the money supply gets too tight, if our universities produce too many Ph.D.s, or for other reasons at which I have hinted in this lecture. But I do not believe there is such a thing as a policy for science as a whole, popular as the concept is. We must have a policy about pollution, ocean resources, food supply, population, water, natural resources and the many other headaches and benefits we can all enumerate. And science, engineering and mathematics – and the research associated with them – will and should contribute to the formulation and implementation of these policies. But that is all: science as a whole is not an activity to be carried on in isolation. It must be part of society's integrated effort to make the world a better place. So the answer to the question posed by Michael Shanks in the last sentence of his article 'Who, in a democratic society, is to give the scientists their marching orders?' is quite simple: democratic society itself and its elected representatives. This is an imperative which applies to all of us, whatever we do, whatever we are, or whatever we wish to be.

9
THE INFAMOUS ROTHSCHILD REPORT

An address to Manchester University Dining Club,
22 February 1972

THERE are two reasons why I am specially happy to come to Manchester this evening: first, because I have a personal connection with the University: and, secondly, because the first Rothschild to come to England, N. M. Rothschild, of Waterloo fame, emigrated from Germany to Manchester. One of the first things he did when he got to Manchester was to make a collection of fabric samples for trade with Germany, which he kept meticulously in what we call his Cotton Book. I thought it might interest you to see this book (opposite) which I think he first started at the end of the eighteenth century. It is about the most precious possession in our family, being the first record of our activities in this country, which have now been going on for somewhat under two hundred years.

Perhaps some of you will be surprised that I have not got two horns and a tail, or a dunce's cap, which you might expect from the correspondence and articles, mainly by scientists, in *The Guardian*, *The Times*, and elsewhere. In reality, I am quite a harmless type and have been a basic research worker for twenty-five years, though inadequately versed, as Dame Albertine Winner has pointed out, in the diplomatic language so characteristic of Whitehall – though I must mention parenthetically that I have simultaneously been accused of writing in 'unintelligible Whitehall jargon'.

With your permission, I don't intend this evening to make a long speech or defensive peroration. Instead, after a few introductory remarks, I thought it better to leave you to speak if you so wish, or ask me questions which I shall do my best to answer.

There have been so many criticisms of my Report that I hardly know where to begin, even in commenting on some of them. But perhaps the most ubiquitous criticism has been that the Report

1802
Feb. 5

Commission from Messrs. Tabard &c & Co
in Paris, for 94 12 Pieces London Printed
Quiltings, agueable to the following Patte
a 5/6/9 to be executed before the 5 March.

1. 2/2
    x   in

2. 1/2
    x

3. 2/2   x in
    x   Piece 32

4. 2/2

5. 2/2
    x

6. 2/2x   Piece 31 in

7. 2/2x   in

8. 1/2

9. 1/2x

10. 4/2x
                                     in
                                     in
11. 2/2   in

12. 2/2

13. 2/2x   in

14. 4/2x
                                     in +
15. 4/2   in 12

16. 1/2x   in

17. 2/2   +0 130

18. 1/2
     √

19. 1/2

20. 2/2x   in

21. 1/2x   in

22. 2/2

23. 2/2   1. 129

24. 4/2x

25. 1/2

26. 1/2   in

27. 1/2x   in

28. 1/2x   in   in 128

29. 1/2

30. 1/2   in

31. 2/2

32. 2/2x   in

33. 4/2

34. 4/2   in +
                  in 12
35. 2/2x

36. 2/2

37. 1/2

38. 2/2x

39. 2/2x   in

40. 2/2x

41. 2/2

42. 2/2x   1 12

43. 2/2
        in 3
44. 1/2

45. 1/2
       x

46. 1/2

47. 4/2   x
          x

48. 1/2
          2/2 x

consists of assertions without explanations or proofs. The most important of these concerns the statement, right at the beginning of my Report, that it is based on the principle that applied R & D must be done on a customer-contractor basis. I do not believe this statement needs any proof or explanation because, as I recently attempted to explain in *Nature*,[14] it is logically self-evident and, being a cautious type, I have had this checked by an excellent professional logician. Let me give you the guts of the argument which, wrongly it seems, I thought so evident as not to warrant mention:

(1) Applied R & D is done by somebody. I call that somebody the contractor, but the contractor could equally well have been called the scientist, the engineer, the mathematician, the research worker, the boffin, or any other word or phrase used to describe or identify that somebody who does the R & D.

(2) Applied R & D is an activity with a potential or actual application. Otherwise the adjective 'applied' would not be used.

(3) An application is a use which in turn requires that there is a user, who could equally well be called a customer, a representative of a customer or user, or even a customer or user surrogate.

That, as they say in the text-books, completes the proof.

I want now to turn to another point, whether applied R & D has a precise meaning or not. I do not equate it with Dainton's tactical research because the latter has a short-term connotation and, indeed, is so interpreted by many of the scientists who have fulminated in public. I believe that everybody in this room knows perfectly well what applied research is and that it is hypocrisy to pretend that one doesn't. Of course, I don't deny that you need the results of basic research to prosecute applied research: or that basic research throws up results of applied interest. And don't forget that applied research also throws up problems of basic interest. I do not deny that there are grey areas, but for goodness sake, don't let's kid ourselves that the phrase applied research does not have a precise meaning. Or that applied research projects are necessarily short-term in nature. Some of you may, perhaps, know that in a recent lecture, I cited the case of a Swiss scientist working for Hoffman La-Roche who worked for twenty years to discover in quick succession the three tranquillizers Librium, Valium and Mogadon. Would you call working for twenty years tactical research?

Many people have stated that the time scale I proposed for the transfer of parts of the Research Councils' financial and programme responsibilities to the appropriate Ministries was too short. In fact, I did not propose any time scale in my Report because I deliberately inserted a condition or requirement, that *no* transfers should be made until and unless the Departments concerned had adequate Chief Scientist organizations. *After* that had occurred, I recommended a limitation on reductions in expenditure, but no limitation on increases. Were you all clear on this point?

People have said that if one has in a Department a Chief Scientist organization, one will merely duplicate the bureaucracy which already exists within the Research Councils. I cannot, of course, say what any Department intends to do: but in my scheme, this is not the case. Were I the Chief Scientist of, for example, the Ministry of Agriculture, the first thing I would do would be to investigate the extent to which I could use the Agricultural Research Council's organization to fulfil the objective of establishing programme priorities. But, of course, the Agricultural Research Council does not contain economists, sociologists, EEC experts and so on. And I believe that in determining national priorities, whether they relate to the agricultural community, the producers of food or the poor old British public which likes to eat, the views of these non-scientific but technically qualified people must be taken into account. That is why the Ministry must, in my view, be concerned with programme priorities.

One of the criticisms I have made of the Research Councils is that in regard to their programmes (not the money they spend) they are not accountable to Parliament directly or through a Minister, because, of course, the Secretary of State for Education & Science cannot answer for the Minister of Agriculture, nor for the Secretary of State for Health and Social Services. I believe this to be wrong. I notice that the President of the Royal Society, when giving evidence to the Select Committee on Science & Technology, claimed that the Research Councils *were* accountable to Parliament by virtue of the fact that they make annual Reports which are laid before Parliament and about which Members of Parliament can, and indeed do, ask questions. But this is not accountability. Having been concerned with the preparation of Annual Reports of the Agricultural Research Council, I know that, quite properly, they are a record of work done and work in progress. What I mean by accountability is the formal requirement to justify programmes, which means they must be annually submitted for approval, not just annually reported on. I don't believe anyone has the right to require this at the present time and, in my evidence to the Select Committee, I cited an example where questions might reasonably be asked, affecting the Medical Research Council.

Of course, this question of accountability is much more relevant to applied than to basic research, because the mechanisms for supporting basic research are well understood and well executed by the scientific community itself. But this is not the case in applied research because I cannot see why scientists should have complete control over the formulation of national objectives requiring research although, of course, they should have a say in that formulation. Ultimately, however, some body must be responsible or accountable for the formulation of these objectives. I don't mind what you call him. Customer may be a bad word, and I would welcome a better and less emotive one. You name it: I'll use it.

One thing has worried me about the reactions of the scientific community to my Report. So many scientists have assumed, wrongly, that I believe the Research Councils have done badly. Otherwise, I would not want to change the set up, they say. The reverse is the case. I know a good deal about the Research Councils and have a great admiration for them. But this does not mean that they cannot do better from a national point of view. As I said to the Select Committee, if I assert that a husband and wife should love each other, it does not imply that husbands and wives don't.

Some of the older scientists in this audience will, I am sure, have had the same experience as me, of looking at their Ph.D. theses or some early paper and thinking 'How could I have written that drivel?' By the same token, there are, in retrospect, several things I regret in my Report. The most important of these is that, in the interests of brevity and, as I thought, readability, I made it too short and wish it had been five or even ten times as long, although I suspect people would then have read it even less carefully than they in fact did. What seemed obvious to me as a research administrator was, evidently, not obvious to the majority of scientists, who have not been research administrators.

May I end by making a prediction without any justification or private information? When the Government comes to consider the reactions to my Report, they will take all the criticisms into consideration. They will say 'There may be something in what Rothschild says: but he does not understand the value of strategic research: the amounts he proposes to transfer are too large: the Research Councils must not reduce their support to the Universities: he has stirred the Research Councils up, which may be a good thing. Therefore we will – ', but I don't know the end of the sentence.

10

ADDRESS TO THE LETCOMBE LABORATORY OF THE AGRICULTURAL RESEARCH COUNCIL

24 August 1973

To my surprise, though few will believe it, the speech which follows caused an uproar of two kinds: first, though it contained nothing which was unknown to the public – and this was confirmed by a poll carried out by a newspaper in which just under 90% of those questioned agreed with the contents of the speech – it attracted considerable Press comment, of which some examples were:

'Stop living in the age of Queen Victoria
BRITAIN BEWARE
Lord Think Tank's 1985 warning'

'ROTHSCHILD: ECONOMISE OR ELSE'

'Serieux avertissement
LORD ROTHSCHILD
INVITE LA GRANDE-BRETAGNE
RENONCER A SES REVES DE GRANDEUR'

The second reason for the uproar was that I forgot (not omitted) to get the speech cleared by the Press Office at No. 10 Downing Street before making it. This was a serious error for which I was, as the Press were told, reprimanded. Naturally, I apologized to the Prime Minister and, as he said in the House of Commons, the matter was then closed. I should have known that all public utterances of civil servants require clearance even if they contain nothing that the public does not know or could not find out; but contrary to widely held belief, I did not deliberately ignore the rules.

A further reason for the uproar was that by a coincidence the Prime Minister was making a speech on the same day in another part of the country. In it he referred to the number of people in the United Kingdom who had colour television sets and other signs of comparative affluence. This, together with the reprimand, gave the Press a second honeymoon:

'TED TO GIVE ROTHSCHILD DRESSING DOWN'

'TOP THINKER ON THE CARPET'

'LORD ROTHSCHILD METTE HEATH IN IMBARAZZO'

It would be surprising and to my mind disheartening if the head of the Government's Think Tank did not from time to time disagree with the Prime Minister and his colleagues. Disagreements did occur from time to time, both before and after the 'Letcombe affair'; and I hope it will not disappoint too many people to learn that both Mr Heath and his successor continue to be friends of mine.

Re-reading what I said, it is somewhat ironical to find that so far from having to wait until 1985 for my gloomy predictions to come true, they have, unfortunately, already done so to a large extent, as the table opposite shows. But I sometimes wonder whether the uproar in the Press was spontaneous or, if not, *who* in fact prompted it.

'Well, you're going to stay in there, Rothschild,
till you come up with the same answer as me!'

SOME INDICATORS OF THE BRITISH ECONOMY
August 1973–October 1976 (or nearest date)

	August 1973	*October 1976*	*%age change*
Dollars to the pound sterling	2.49 (24.8.73)	1.78 (24.8.76)	−29
Unemployment*	590,000	1,300,000	+120
Industrial Output (1970=100)	111.0	102.3	−8
Wage rates (July 1972=100)	115.4	217.4	+88

CHANGE ON A YEAR EARLIER

Retail Prices Index (1970=100)	128.8	216.8	+68
Industrial Production (1970=100)	110.4	102.6	−7
Money supply (m3)	+27	+13	+49

£BILLION

Gross Domestic Product:			
current prices	62.50	104.25	+67
constant 1970 prices	48.25	47.75	−1
Currency reserves ($ billion)	6628	4703	−29
Current account balance	−0.50	−2.75	−450
Trade balance	−2.50	−4.50	−125
Total outstanding national debt (March)	37	56.50	+53
Public sector borrowing (fiscal year)	4.50 (1973-4)	11 (est. 1976-7)	+144

* UK seasonally adjusted, excluding students and school-leavers.
Note. Some of these figures may require modification by the time this book is published.

WHEN Dr Scott Russell invited me to make a brief address to you to inaugurate your new Seminar Room, I asked him on what subject I should talk, reminding him that my field was very limited. He thought some general aspect of research would be acceptable.

Nothing is more boring and irritating than listening to someone plaintively explaining why he has been misunderstood and therefore not loved by his critics. So I won't dwell on those issues.

But I do think it may be useful to say a little about some general issues affecting this country which in fact prompted me to say what I did, deliberately in stark language rather than the circumlocutory half-truths and understatements normally, but often unjustly, expected from a Civil Servant writing a report. These general issues can be summed up by ventilating a fear I have, which I believe has virtually nothing to do with the politics of the left, right, or centre, about the future of this country. From the vantage point of the Cabinet Office, it seems to me that unless we take a very strong pull at ourselves and give up the idea that we are one of the wealthiest, most influential and important countries in the world – in other words that Queen Victoria is still reigning – we are likely to find ourselves in increasingly serious trouble. To give just one unpalatable example, in 1985 we shall have half the economic weight of France or Germany, that is to say, the GNP of the United Kingdom will be half that of France or Germany, and about equal to that of Italy. Two things can be said about this proposition. First, that Britain, or for all I know, Italy, is a very nice place to live in, in spite of the things we grouse about, such as giant articulated lorries and the festering centres of urban deprivation. Why fuss so much about the economic indicators? The second comment is this: why are you so confident that we cannot catch up, even by 1985? How can you, who are not even a professional economist, and God knows they are not so reliable, be so dogmatic?

I would like to deal briefly with these two points and then, equally briefly, with their implications.

Let us accept that, by and large, this is a pleasant country to live in and, judging by the foreign tourist density in Cambridge, this view is not a reflection of our insularity, but is shared by Germans, Frenchmen, Dutchmen, Japanese, Americans and many others. Nevertheless, we have obligations which, independent of our political beliefs, we should and are going to honour. I am not thinking of grandiose world obligations, however important some people may think these are; but of obligations at home, to do with the Elderly, the Infirm, the Sick and, in general, what are nowadays called the Disadvantaged. The lower our GNP, the greater the percentage of it which has to be spent on the Disadvantaged and the less there is available for other important matters, such as capital investment in the Nationalized Industries, reducing taxation in spite of the passion some people have for increasing it, getting a better rail service, stopping those giant articulated lorries thundering through country villages by building by-passes, providing theatres and museums in many parts of Britain instead of only a few large towns, and so on, whatever your particular fancy may be.

I turn now to the question, can't we do better? A number of politicians would, I believe, question my second proposition that, by 1985, we shall only have half the economic weight of France or Germany. Whether they would dispute it for what I might call political reasons, or because they believe subconsciously that we are still in the Victorian era, or because they really know better, is difficult to discern. (I do know some who actually agree with me.) 'Do you not realize', some have said, 'that France is in a very delicately balanced condition? Do you not remember the student riots? What about the Algerians in Marseille? Do you really not know that countries just can't keep up their high levels of economic growth indefinitely?' There are two remarks to be made about these objections: first, even if the economic growth of France and Germany does, in fact, slow down, I think one can show that we are not going to catch up. But the second comment qualifies the first – there is a chance that we could do very well. But the realization of this chance depends on something that seems very difficult to achieve in this country. It is the knowledge that our difficulties and dangers are as severe and ominous as they were in World War II, though, of course, of a different sort. They are not to do with systematic destruction from the air,

93

which the Battle of Britain prevented. They are not to do, I hope, with the imposition of a Fascist régime in Britain. But the dangers we are facing require us to do something very difficult and which we seem to find harder than several other countries, that is, to have now the mentality we had during World War II. I don't suppose there are many people here who remember Churchill's broadcasts to the nation, telling us about the dangers, the rewards and the duties of everyone in the country; and I don't believe our attitude towards those dangers was entirely due to Churchill, though of course he marvellously helped. In those days, everyone got down to doing what the country needed him or her to do. My old friend Alan Hodgkin stopped his epoch-making research on conduction in nerves and became a distinguished and highly successful radar specialist. I am not suggesting for a moment that such action is needed now. But I do think that somehow or other, every man and woman in the country must be made aware of the dangers and difficulties ahead and of the need to contribute to their solution, even if that necessitates giving up a small fraction of the freedom of action and decision which are more appropriate to the reign of Queen Victoria than to the present time. It is just no good for the Medical Research Council to assert its right to complete freedom of scientific action provided that action comes under some appropriately worded umbrella; and the same applies to the Natural Environment Council. We have not the means, resource-wise or money-wise, to accept that all Research Council-funded research is a cultural activity analogous to the support of the Arts.

As a matter of fact, the Agricultural Research Council never took that line in my days, which was why, you may think perversely, I sometimes took up the opposite position. I remember Solly Zuckerman and I trying very hard merely to study the extent to which the ARC's research was relevant to British food production. (Of course, neither of us was so stupid as to think the word 'relevant' was easy to interpret.) We didn't do too well in this study and were both rather frustrated. Now, the ARC has gone a long way down the road in what might be called identification and diagnosis. How far it will be possible, and how long it will take, to move into the field of treatment is an interesting question and one worthy of much intensive thought and discussion. The

ARC is specially well placed in this respect as the Chief Scientist of the MAFF is one of your 'old boys'.

To sum up, if we are to solve or even ameliorate the problems and dangers we are facing, there must be a major national change of orientation. We have to think twice about the desirability of courses of action which, in the distant past, were ours by right. We have to realize that we have neither the money nor the resources to do all those things we would like to do and so often feel we have the right to do.

But, of course, this is very difficult. When you have 1 million unemployed it is not easy to scrap the Concorde even if that were a good idea, and put another 25,000 men out of work quite apart from the financial penalties of breaking a Treaty. It is not easy to scrap a new form of surface transport. It is not easy to stop thinking it quite reasonable to have four different sorts of nuclear reactors on the go at the same time. Perhaps you will think of some other examples from the world of science and R & D. But if we don't grasp this nettle, we shall not solve those difficulties I mentioned earlier which, as sure as eggs are eggs, are with us now.

THINKING

What is it? How is it best done?

Lecture at the University of Newcastle upon Tyne,
25 October 1973

BEING paid to think, it is, perhaps, natural to think about thinking. What *is* thinking? How is it best done? Thinking about thinking is not easy. I would go further and confess that it is extremely hard work. But for me, it has one major advantage. Thinking, or even thinking about thinking, is not forbidden in Estacode, the Civil Service Bible.

It may be best to begin with a traditional distinction between two types of thinking and between two powers that mind possesses. They are analytical and synthetic thinking. Analytical thinking is directed to problems that are already formulated more or less explicitly and that are susceptible to a solution obtained by methods more or less in regular use. The virtues of analytical thinking are first, lucidity and, secondly, the habit of incisively distinguishing those elements in the problem which can be distinguished, so that the problem becomes open to solution by taking the elements one by one. The powers of mind involved are those that you would expect to find typically, so far as practical affairs are concerned, in a Chancery lawyer or a good chess player at Club level. Both the explicitness of the problem and the known regularity of methods of solution are essential to purely analytical thinking. If the problem or set of problems has not been delineated in any definite way, or if the various methods of finding a solution are always open to challenge, then powers of intellectual analysis cannot by themselves be sufficient to find the solution.

For analytical thinking in its pure form, which requires the power to distinguish the elements of a problem and to see the relation between them, the first necessity is the power to direct attention for several minutes continuously to a set of questions which are related, without allowing one's attention to stray;

in other words, concentration, which implies that one's mind is closed to externalities. This power is well described by Nabokov in a novel called *The Defence*,[15] which is about thinking in chess.

The answer to the question 'How is it (analytical thinking) best done?' is, according to conventional wisdom – which there is no reason to challenge – practise sustaining attention on a technical problem, with a known method or methods of solution, and notice how the length of time you can allot to continuous thinking varies with your state of health and physical condition. Nobody, I believe, knows what constitutes 'continuous thinking' as the phrase is used here, whether he is a philosopher or a psychologist. But one does have a rough notion, in one's own case, of when one's attention begins to stray, and one can learn a technique of observing the fluctuations of concentration. Logicians of sound reputation certainly develop unusual powers of concentration in rather the same way as chess players.

There is an unfortunate tendency in ordinary thought and language to identify thinking with analytical thought. As I hope to persuade you, this is an error. Analytical thinking is a specific kind of thought and a kind which is a very general, though perhaps not universal, ingredient in all high level and original thought. There is also a tendency in contemporary language to ascribe analytical thinking to a faculty called the intellect, but the allocation of this particular faculty to analytical thinking is not general in history. But let us accept the allocation for a moment. Then the traditional contrasting faculty which sustains thought of the other specific kind has been called, since the eighteenth century, imagination. Of course, I do not mean imagination in the sense of the power of entertaining or producing images; but rather the power of synthetic thinking. I must now make the contrast. Synthetic thinking is typically required when the thinker is not presented with an already formulated question or problem, or set of questions and problems. Instead, it is required when in a difficulty or when, beginning work, a man* needs gradually to make clear to himself, to have made clear to him, what his difficulty is, how it is best realized or expressed, what is the nature of the work on which he is engaged, or what his purpose is. I find, rather too often for my liking, that I frequently do not

* Or woman, of course, here and elsewhere.

know the answer to the question 'What am I trying to think about?' It is *something*, but I am not clear where I am going nor where I want to go. I need help from someone cleverer (or more intelligent).

Traditionally, the contrast between the analytical and the synthetic has been made by saying that analytical intelligence is concerned with finding the most rational and well-ordered means towards an end already stated: synthetic intelligence is called upon when there is vagueness or uncertainty or unresolved complexity about ends. But this is too simple a contrast and not general enough. Broadly speaking, synthetic intelligence has to invent the terms in which future analytical thinking is to be conducted, and also to invent, or to impose, new criteria of success. It is the power to make connections between disparate subject matters and problems which ordinary able analytical thinkers have not associated in their thought. The great mathematician, von Neumann, was an example of an imaginative, synthetic thinker who might wrongly be supposed to be a master only of analytical thinking. He had the extremely rare capability of making connections between, for example, welfare economics, traditional theories of gambling and probability, new principles of rational choice and several branches of mathematics, all of which had previously been investigated more or less separately. In discussion he was always putting ideas from distinct and apparently unrelated disciplines together and then asking whether sense or nonsense resulted. It is the essence of this kind of thinking that one should knowingly be running the risk of arriving at nonsense. There has to be the kind of vagueness of purpose and vagueness about the criteria of success that one notices when some artist begins to paint or draw. The typical virtues attached to this kind of thinking are what has often been called 'thoughtfulness', 'originality' and 'inventiveness'. The thoughtful, original or inventive man is not the man who solves a complex problem elegantly and fast: but rather the person who changes the terms in which a problem is discussed in such a way that new lines of argument, connecting hitherto unrelated notions, are opened up. This was conspicuously the power which the young Bertrand Russell had in writing about philosophy and, particularly, philosophy and logic. He asked questions about, for example, the nature of numbers and of classes, which had been asked by clever men with analytical minds for many centuries. But he proposed drastically simple answers by altering the concepts from which the problems were derived. In addition, of course, he possessed analytical powers of the highest order, in the sense that he was able to work out the implications of his proposals to very remote conclusions and foresee the paradoxes and contradictions to which his suggestions might lead. But his description in his autobiography of the exhaustion which thought produced in him is not entirely a description of the exhaustion which the complex working out of complex problems produces; it is also a description of whole months when he as it were stared at a central logical difficulty which seemed to stand in the way of all his results and possible solutions. What he had to have was an idea, in the sense in which one might suddenly have an idea in the Archimedes way and shout Eureka. He described such moments. The point about such thinking is that one cannot use a regular method of tracing connections and a regular technique of checking the reliability of one's results, as one can to some degree in all analytical thinking. What is needed instead is that one should step back from the formulation of the problem and methods of solution that immediately suggest themselves, and start to combine and re-combine elements in an entirely new order.

Most people who have been in this sense thoughtful and, at a higher level, original and inventive, have stressed that ideas, in the relevant sense, often come when concentration is relaxed and when one is engaged on some more or less routine and unexacting work connected with the subjects in hand. It does not seem that concentration is either necessary or sufficient for the kind of thought which enables one to break away from orthodox methods of solution and re-formulate problems in ways that open up new evidence and new lines of argument. Therefore, in answering the question 'How best is it done?' one is in rather a false position, precisely because this kind of thinking necessitates the escape from regular techniques. There are certain maxims which can be found repeated at different times and which seem to have force. First, that this kind of thoughtfulness depends on one not being afraid of, nor discouraged from, asking crude, simple, fundamental questions. One must have circumstances in which one can ask oneself and others questions which may have an embarrassingly simple answer, and one must try varying methods of enquiry or of work in a way that may also lead to embarrassingly feeble results.

Not all thinking is in words or mathematical symbols, whether of the analytical or synthetic kind. It may be in images. Equally, not all problems and tasks which require thought are best formulated in language or in mathematical symbols. An architect, a sculptor or a doctor may think in a variety of ways that cannot easily be reduced to the type of verbal and mathematical thinking with which academic people are most familiar. The element of thought when a good painter is painting a portrait, or a good poet is writing a poem, or a good musician is composing, is the same as when Fischer is addressing himself to a serious chess game, or Dirac to a problem in theoretical physics. In all these cases there is need both of synthetic thought, which transforms the apparent problems into new, unforeseen problems, and of analytical thinking that tests suggested results by looking clearly and sharply at the outcome and noticing incoherences and failures of connection. One can also think of men who have had the kind of thoughtfulness associated with problem-changing and also had relatively weak analytical powers. Their work will tend towards vagueness, lack of definition, suggestiveness, but they may be of use to others. Much more common, obviously, is the work produced at a high level of clear arrangement, adequate supporting evidence and absence of contradiction; these are the hall marks of analytical intelligence. Putting, therefore, the two kinds of thought together, and taking account of the polymorphism of thought, that is the width of range of material to which it is applied, one must conclude as follows: there is no entirely detachable power of thought; thought in a given person is directed towards certain subject matters which have an emotional significance, directly or indirectly, for that person. The most general precept for improving powers of thought must surely be that the subject matter – buildings for an architect, chess for the chess player – is genuinely and deeply rooted in the interests of the person concerned. It is perfectly true that there are analytical intelligences, particularly of the logical kind and also in mathematics at a certain level, which are open to being switched to different subject matters more or less indifferently, rather as one might use a vacuum cleaner on a variety of different carpets. (The Government's Think Tank must be mainly, but not exclusively, of this sort.) If one is asked about the nature of thought, and methods of thinking better, the generality of the question leads one to take as a paradigm of the thinker the analytical intelligence alone. This is unfortunate. If pressed to be practical, I would say that the best way of improving powers of thought, either for an individual or a group, is for that individual or group to make sure he or they are really interested in the questions and in the work they suppose themselves to be interested in. This is particularly necessary if thoughtfulness of the second kind, and therefore real inventiveness, is to be developed. The subject matter has to be moving about in one's head in unconcentrated moments and more or less all the time, so that the separated elements of a confused problem combine and re-combine in one's head in a kind of Brownian motion. Then a certain combination may be recognized, in spite of its apparently random origin, as a Eureka situation. It is quite remarkable how much evidence there is in autobiographical writings of men who made quite dissimilar inventions which testifies to this.

What is thinking? How is it best done? How is it best developed and how can it be improved and made more effective? I shall deal first with the 'more effective' part of the question.

It is certain that we shall need to know the physical structures on which thought depends before we can methodically improve our powers of thought. We shall need to know and understand how these powers work, in the same way and in the same degree that we know and understand the working of our sense organs such as the eye and the ear. Until this physiological knowledge becomes available, we are guessing or, at best, relying on the kind of empirical knowledge that the day-to-day meteorologists use, when we enunciate maxims about the improvement of thought. The first maxim, and a well-established one, is that we think effectively when we have extended a form of knowledge that we have acquired, and successfully used, from one subject matter to another. For example, we may extend the laws of chance originally applied to gambling situations or in actuarial calculations to natural processes, and find we are thinking effectively: in other words, that our way of thinking about, for example, a biological process does divide the phenomenon into intelligible patterns with which we are already familiar and does enable us to state very general truths about the phenomenon in a compact, memorable and manageable way. In general we may successfully extend to social phenomena and mental states models of reasoning which have proved successful in studying very general truths about physical realities. But at a certain point, which we are unable to predict, this extrapolation of established successful ways of thinking breaks down when applied to the new subject matter. It is, for example, notorious that the attempt to formulate sociological laws using roughly the same form as the laws of dynamics has led to uninteresting results. It has proved so far useless, or near-useless, to interpret social changes according to these well-established patterns of thought. This also happens at unpredicted points in understanding physical structures; for example, mechanical models of the functioning of the brain, which depend upon localizing function and looking for uniform connections between the localized functions, have proved to be an unprofitable way of thinking about this particular type of physical object.

Therefore the contrast I suggested earlier between analytical and synthetic thinking could be restated as a contrast on the one hand between extending habits of thought which have proved well adapted to relatively well-understood new subject matters; and, on the other, synthetic hand, the change to a new scheme of explanation and a new model of understanding, when passing to a new subject matter that has proved recalcitrant to established ways of thought. We are in need of an empirical theory of knowledge which tells us what kind of problems of an urgent or important kind we can expect to solve with our present habits of thought and scientific resources. Lacking this empirical theory of knowledge, we in fact solve problems which yield to established methods and dismiss as insoluble those problems that we do not, unless there happens to be an imaginative thinker, a von Neumann around. This is very plain in history when one recalls the Newtonian physiologies and the Newtonian theories of society, and the Newtonian biologies which followed Newton, or the cybernetic models of social change, or mental functioning, or foreign policy, which followed Norbert Wiener. This is why futurology, at least the American if not the French variety with its content of sociological and anthropological assumptions, is a dubious intellectual enterprise, for it involves projecting into the future not only the sciences and technologies in which we are currently most interested and which are being rapidly developed, but also the habits of mind and the type of explanation we have found adequate in our present state of knowledge. Futurology would be a less dubious activity if we had a general theory of the development of human powers of understanding, particularly understanding of phenomena that are complex relative to our present knowledge. Then we might be in a position to predict that it would pay us to neglect certain new, flourishing lines of enquiry and also to neglect certain intractable problems, either scientific or social, and turn to precisely those problems we are now equipped to solve and which are also important. Each intelligent individual does acquire by experience, at least by the time he is thirty, a fairly definite, empirical sense of what kind of problem he is capable of thinking about effectively and whether he has a chance of innovating, or no chance at all. It is more difficult to develop such a self-consciousness in the community among those who are expected to solve social and political problems; but it ought not to be altogether impossible. We do at least know in, for example, a field of study like transport that we have no general method of examining and designing transport systems that will satisfy human needs, while we do have methods of devising particular forms of transport effectively but without the ability to combine them into an effective whole: by contrast those who work in this field probably can say whether they are likely to find a clear way of thinking about the transport system of the country as a whole, within the next five or ten years. They should ask themselves the question, 'Do we have the conceptual apparatus, and some established practice of thought which will help us, and is there a person or group of persons who have got some way along the path, or are we just applying routine methods of thought to the problem without any reason to believe that the methods fit the problem?' An empirical theory of knowledge would cause Research Councils and Government research establishments invariably to ask themselves the question, 'Is this a problem for which I have invented, or am inventing, methods that fit exactly this problem, or am I just extrapolating already successful methods of thought?' It would not be difficult to recall a number of national projects whose fate reflects this lack of an empirical theory of knowledge.

But the concentration on system can also be misleading when it is taken out of its original place and applied, for example, to social groups. Whether it is misleading or not is again learned only by experience. But in advance of experience the art of thought principally consists in being ready to change gear from one scheme of explanation, or convention of interpretation, to another, at the first signs of a failure to explain and interpret clearly when the subject matter changes. Philosophically, the position is more complicated than this, because the distinctions between different subject matters are themselves a product of our schemes of explanation and conventions of interpretation, or, in a very general sense, of our language. Therefore the opposition between the subject matter or the phenomena and our habits of thought in interpreting them is rather naive. Nevertheless there are inherited dividing lines which must be used in marking off different subject matters; and it is legitimate to speak of subject matters about which we know that we know virtually nothing in any definite way, just as there are subject matters over whose complexities we have a clear mastery. The original thinker changes the boundaries by suddenly discarding the habit of interpretation, or changing a style of thinking, as painters change styles of paintings. This now happens in all the sciences and it should happen in Government planning. I do not think that the art of thought, while physiology is deficient or lacking, can do much more than warn of the necessity of trying a change of gear, that is, of trying to look for new models of interpretation, when thinking about social problems. This amounts to a distrust of too great a trust in analytical methods in the sense in which a Chancery barrister, a chess player or a systems analyst employs analytical methods.

I return now to the question, 'What is thinking?' It is natural to think of thinking as being a device for the rapid adaptation of behaviour within the species without changing the genetic material. The important feature of thought is that it allows very rapid and varied adaptations of behaviour within narrow limits to be tried without transmitting a big cost to the next generation. It must be remembered that any thought is potentially something communicated to other members of the species. Thought is potentially public and publishable, involving as it does a language or some other established symbolic system. Therefore the extension of thought, or the extension of language, is an acquisition to the species, in the same sense that an extra limb or a tool would be. Thought is transmittable through the language-learning capacity, and each child inherits a capital of ready-made thought capacity which has proved helpful in adaptation to new situations. Therefore thought is the means by which social diversity can be produced by diversity of language and cultural tradition, and the species, considered as a whole, tries out different ways of life experimentally. This is the natural way of viewing thought, by analogy with the development of sensory organs and of limbs. This may be too simple a conception, because we must admit that most of our thinking is not within consciousness and that we are not aware of its steps. It is therefore not entirely clear that all our thoughts are communicable and potentially public. What I called the natural way of viewing thought applies to conscious and disciplined thought, which has a statable goal.

It is always profitable to think of thought by analogy with the senses and to think of the brain, which is the instrument of thought, in analogy with the eye. The really difficult problem is the suggestion of mystery about the functioning of the organ of thought, namely the brain. It may seem odd and paradoxical to suggest that it is a lack of understanding of physiology which is holding us up in thinking about thinking. But I believe this to be true. I do not believe we can have an adequate theory of thought and of knowledge unless we know in rough outline what sort of physical system the brain has, when understood in terms of its functions. But of course I have no idea whether such understanding of the functioning of the brain is attainable by us with our present models of explanation and conventions of interpretation.

There are, therefore, two separate tasks for anyone who designs an instrument for thought, whether that instrument is himself or a set of persons whose assignment is to think: first, that he should both test and also practise powers of concentration in a material which has to be their material: that is to say, in words and mathematical symbols for most civil servants and most academic persons, but not necessarily for most architects and most town planners. Secondly, that he should discover what material of thought, in the sense in which words are the material of thought, most delight a person whom one is to develop or use as a thinker, including oneself.

Very many, and perhaps most, people believe that certain things delight and interest them, when in fact they do not. The test is what people's minds turn to in an undisciplined way when they are not answering to social needs or stimuli from the environment but are rather letting their minds do their own thinking, as Mozart described in his letters. Consequently, I would not collect a body of detached thinkers for any serious purposes other than the solution of already formulated problems by methods which are not altogether new. One needs in a set of persons genuinely diverse interests, for example, as between mathematical arguments and verbal presentation, between abstract and factual reasoning, and so on. As for myself, I am resigned to the conclusion that one is only capable of thinking usefully and seriously about a quite narrow range of subject matters, which are those in which the mere material, that is words to me, abstract entities to logicians and mathematicians, are in themselves delightful. Then one has a chance of being able to concentrate, as is necessary for analytical thinking, and to let apparently random ideas develop, as is necessary for imaginative thinking.

Humour can contribute to thinking in the sense that play, and playing with ideas, allows the mind to stray across open ground rather than follow already established paths. Humour arises from incongruities and these are inhibited by severely practical and analytical thinking. The metaphor of straying and of paths may be illuminating and not just a metaphor. It is certain that one uses a store of collateral or subconscious information and ideas in any process of thought that is serious and difficult, without being aware either of the extent or of the origin of the information and the ideas on which one is very rapidly drawing. It would be literally impossible to mention all the information and all the ideas that are activated while one is thinking. The phenomenon of intuition, which is well-known in experts in crafts and arts, illustrates the use of collateral information and ideas which are not articulated; intuition notoriously also plays a part in the sciences, in mathematics and in intellectual games. Philosophers have long had the habit, particularly if they are empiricist philosophers, of referring to intuition as abbreviated inference. The importance of this doctrine is to be found in the suggestion that it makes about inference: namely, that inference is sometimes a process that is open to inspection while it occurs and then can be described as a sequence of steps. But that inference should be so overt and perceptible is the exception and not the rule. Generally speaking, inference occurs below the level of self-consciousness and without the separate inferential steps being articulated. Not only this, but usually, the sequence of steps in the inference cannot be reconstructed as a sequence of steps even in retrospect. There are various ways of establishing this conclusion. One interesting way is to investigate the inferences that one makes in identifying something by sight, whether that something is a person, a building, or an object of a specific kind. If this is done carefully and under something like laboratory conditions, one will find that the indefinite variety of possibilities is narrowed down, and eliminated, by the use of an immense variety of stored information, about which one is not even usually aware, both as regards its existence and source. Possibilities are eliminated at enormous speed, just as a chess player does when looking five moves ahead. This is how the mind is always functioning during its waking hours, because this is how the brain functions; but we do not of course know how this functioning of the brain is brought about; we do not know the mechanism by which the stored collateral information and ideas are activated, nor the method of storage. But we do know that the mind naturally meets any perceptual problems by trying the normal hypothesis and will even distort and misread data to fit them into it. Only in extreme circumstances, or with specially trained observers, will the mind be ready to accept that an unusual conjunction of phenomena is there to be perceived. Consequently the mind may be said, not unfairly, to be designed to assimilate the inputs to which it is exposed into certain standard patterns; this has an evolutionary advantage in producing high average results in appropriate quick response, taking the species as a whole and given a moderately stable environment. The cost of this evolutionary advantage is an inbuilt tendency to overlook differences that do not generally have a significance for the species as a whole, and those that have only recently become important, from the survival point of view, of the whole species. Thus a very elaborate training is needed to develop powers of discrimination that are not genetically inbuilt because they have not so far conferred a high average advantage. The natural way provided for developing these powers of discrimination is play: for play is a highly specialized type of activity directed towards a goal that is in some way superfluous to needs, gratuitous, and not economic. So children and young animals develop their physical and other powers in play, and similarly play with ideas is the normal way of side-tracking the habitual responses of the mind. For example, epigrams give pleasure because they reverse, as it were, a normal muscular contraction and give one a surprise which is like toppling over or tripping up. In order to give intuition, as abbreviated or accelerated inference, a good chance of success, one needs to loosen the set connections called rules of relevance, which will lead the mind to respond in one of a narrow range of possible ways to a given problem. One needs to try the chance of collateral knowledge and ideas from a wide range of different sources being brought to bear on a problem with which this information and these ideas are not usually associated. This is the principal benefit one gets from discussing possibilities in a large group of persons. It is, I suppose, a simple proposition in any theory of probability that a wider range of connections is liable to be touched off in one person's head if seven or eight people are experimenting with information and ideas at the top of their voices simultaneously.

There is, therefore, a kind of opposition which some would unhelpfully and irritatingly call dialectical, between drawing to the fullest possible extent on an uncharted range of collateral information and ideas, and at the same time preserving concentration on a single problem. This opposition may even have some sort of physiological model as its base. At least it seems to me that the art of thinking, in intellectual enquiries but not the imaginative arts, largely consists in combining the advantages of concentration and dispersed material. From a practical point of view it is most important that one cannot tell by introspection whether one is thinking effectively or not; one can only judge by results. By the same token one cannot tell how good one's sight is until one's sight is tested. There is nothing strange in the fact that some of one's most effective thinking takes place at times when one would not expect this to happen, and when one has not prepared the occasion, and even when one does not know at the time that one is thinking about the problem to which one in fact then finds a useful solution. Lastly, it is not to be assumed that all thinking is problem-solving, or even that the best of it is. Much of it is problem-identifying or problem-changing, and some of it is not properly expressed in the framework of problem-solution at all. This is no less true of thought about social, political, and economic issues as about thought in the sciences, mathematics and philosophy.

There are endless rather terrifying stories about how the great do it – rightly or wrongly I deliberately avoid the word think. Henri Poincaré, one of the world's greatest mathematicians, who, when at the height of his powers, agreed to submit to the Binet psychological tests and came out rated as an imbecile, had this to say about how he did it, whatever 'it' may be:

> 'For a fortnight I struggled to prove that no functions analogous to those I have since called Fuchsian functions could exist; I was then very ignorant. Every day I sat down at my work table where I spent an hour or two; I tried a great number of combinations and arrived at no result. One evening, contrary to my custom, I took black coffee; I could not go to sleep, ideas swarmed up in clouds; I sensed them clashing until, as it were, a pair would hook together to form a stable combination. By morning, I had established the existence of a class of Fuchsian functions . . .
>
> I had only to write up the results, which took me a few hours.'[16]

So according to Poincaré, your subconscious, unconscious, subliminal or collateral mind not only stores information; it can also scrutinize, analyse and permute that information and reject all but the useful combinations.

Here and there in this lecture I have expressed some views on how to think better. But so far as synthetic or creative thinking –

the most elusive and interesting – is concerned, perhaps the best advice is: find out what is *your* black coffee; is it Mozart, Art Tatum (like me), a bus trip (like Kékulé), sitting uncomfortably in a pub (like my mentor, Hampshire), a journey in the Tube (like my colleague, Ross), or gazing out of the window. Once you have made *that* discovery, creative thinking may become a reality. The rest will come with practice and determination.

But, as so often is the case, the Bible has the last word:

'The mind toils in one place, while God toils for it in another.'[17]

12

THE GOVERNMENT'S
THINK TANK AND
THE NATION'S BUSINESS

Address at St George's House, Windsor Castle
to the Windsor Consultation for Senior Church Leaders,
7 October 1974

This audience, which might be described as 'Middle Management' with a sprinkling of 'Directors' such as the Dean of Windsor
and the Bishops of Dudley, Woolwich and Oxford, was one of the
most intelligent and receptive I have met. At the end of the discussion which followed my address I said it seemed to me that their
policy objectives were sufficiently unclear to warrant their
establishing a Think Tank and that, if it was thought suitable, I
was available on a part-time basis.

As I am sure you know, very strict regulations exist to prevent
retired Civil Servants, and particularly senior ones, from saying
anything which has not been authorized about their Whitehall
work or, indeed, their Whitehall life if, as is so often the case, this
involves official information. In fact, one of the earliest signs that
one is on one's way out is not, as one might perhaps expect,
someone saying 'sorry you're going' or some other platitude, but
the receipt of a document from those in charge of what I would
call administration, containing minatory and, I assume, intentionally frightening injunctions, of which the following is an
example and one which I am expected, indeed compelled I
imagine, to sign:

'I am liable to be prosecuted if either in the UK or abroad I
communicate either orally or in writing, including publication
of a speech, lecture, radio or television broadcast, or in the
Press or in book form or otherwise, to any unauthorized
person, any information acquired as a result of my appointment

(save such as has already officially been made public) unless I have previously obtained official sanction in writing of the Department by which I was appointed.'

Sir Burke (now Lord) Trend, until recently Secretary of the Cabinet, told me that though I could admit that the Government's Think Tank took an *interest* in certain subjects (apart from a few sensitive ones), I could in no circumstances admit that we had written a report on any of them.*

So any relationship between what I say and the reality of having been a 'Crown Servant' for the last four or so years is, with the exception of what is public knowledge, wholly coincidental.

I do not know how many of you know what the Government's Think Tank is. Lord Plowden was, I think, the first person to discern the need to establish a group of people, who might or might not be Civil Servants, who, located at the centre, would render independent advice to the Government on major policy issues. 'Independent advice' meant advice independent of Government Departments (though not of their knowledge and information – that would be impossible), and of particular political beliefs. The accent was to be on multi- or trans-departmental issues and not on problems requiring immediate action. Indexation and the Social Services are examples of what, perhaps, Lord Plowden had in mind. The Conservative Party latched on to this concept which, in mid-1970, was enshrined, in characteristically sonorous prose, in a White Paper, Command 4506. But a brilliant member of the Think Tank summarized our functions in what I believe to be more precise, more comprehensible, more accurate and certainly more terse language. He said that the functions of the Central Policy Review Staff, the correct but seldom used name of the Think Tank, were:

'Sabotaging the over-smooth functioning of the machinery of Government.

Providing a Central Department which has no departmental axe to grind but does have overt policy status and which can attempt a synoptic view of policy.

Provide a Central reinforcement for those Civil Servants in

---

* The secrecy surrounding the Think Tank's activities may now have been relaxed.

Whitehall who are trying to retain their creativity and not be totally submerged in the bureaucracy.

Try to devise a more rational system of decision-making between competing programmes.

Advise the Cabinet collectively, and the Prime Minister, on major issues of policy relating to the Government's Strategy.

Focus the attention of Ministers on the right questions to ask about their own colleagues' business.

Bring in ideas from the outside world.'

I referred earlier to problems requiring immediate action not being the concern of the Tank. This reservation has, potentially, been of great value to our opponents, enabling them to enjoin us to get back into the 1990's and not interfere in the day-to-day management of Government. This has led, periodically, to a peculiarly sterile argument about the difference between short, medium and long-term work with which I will not weary you except to say that a decision taken now, that is in the short-term, may have very long-term consequences, up to the end of the century for example. The inordinately delayed decision on nuclear reactors, so often mentioned in the Press and in which the Tank was much interested, came into the category of a subject requiring urgent decision: but with effects that will still be felt in the year 2000.

Briefly, the Tank consists of sixteen or so graduates of both sexes, whose average age was thirty-seven in May (thirty-five without me), with a small – too small – supporting staff. As every 'professional' costs somewhat more than £10,000 a year it follows that the annual cost of the Think Tank is more than £200,000. You may be surprised at this figure because it differs from some given in Parliament; but that is due to my training in a previous industrial incarnation, where we were made to know, very clearly, what each person *really* costs which, of course, includes many things such as the rental value of the square footage one occupies and other on-costs, such as travel, consultants' fees and transport, quite apart from salaries.

Under the previous administration the Think Tank's work could be classified under three headings:

Six-monthly review of the Government's Strategy, to the
Cabinet and, separately, to Middle and Junior Ministers.
Special Studies requested or approved by the Cabinet.
Collective Briefs.

Though I will say a little about the first two of these in a few
moments, I shall begin by explaining the phrase Collective
Briefs, because in a way, it is these that give the Think Tank a
great deal of freedom and which, from time to time, cause
irritation. The phrase refers to the fact that the Think Tank can
intervene, often, but not necessarily, by means of a short report
to the Cabinet or a Cabinet Committee, on virtually any subject
it likes, with the reservation, of course, that uninformed or useless
intervention would very soon effect the demise of the Think Tank.

Of course, in order to intervene one must set up an early
warning system or intelligence service to spot the subjects which
are likely to come to Ministers, and this is one of the reasons why
the Think Tank must be located in the Cabinet Office because the
Cabinet Secretariat is better informed than any other part of
Whitehall as to what Ministers will have to attend to in the future.
It would be no good us waiting until a departmental or ministerial
report, for example on the Education of Handicapped Children,
is produced, because it may not be issued until forty-eight hours
before the Cabinet or Cabinet Committee meeting, by which
time it is, of course, out of the question to attempt a critical
analysis. We therefore had to maintain what might almost be
called a portfolio of Collective Briefs which could be quickly
updated for use when necessary.

For a while Departments were quite allergic to our Collective
Briefs because they provided an independent analysis, by a group
of people uncontaminated by years of Whitehall experience, of
the subject under consideration. This allergy was evidenced by
statements or accusations that Think Tank briefs were 'naive' or
'superficial'. Sometimes, perhaps, they were (occasionally on
purpose); but the frequency of the accusations was significantly
greater than the frequency of their veracity. More recently,
Departments have realized that the CPRS's Collective Briefs may
be useful to them in furthering the cause they foster. On occasions,
even, Departments have thought it a good thing for the Think

Tank to put a cause up independently from the Department normally concerned.

The programme of work which used to be handed down to us by the Cabinet tended to be concerned with subjects of trans-departmental interest; because obviously the Government would go to the appropriate Department about a subject which was its sole concern; but it turns out, of course, that many subjects which superficially seem to 'belong' to one Department in fact do not. A good, if obvious example, on which the Think Tank spent a lot of time and effort, was Concorde. One might think that, under the previous administration, this was the sole responsibility of the Department of Trade & Industry and now, of the Department of Industry. But this is not the case. The Foreign Office is deeply involved in Concorde because it is a collaborative venture with France. The Department of the Environment is involved because of noise problems: and so, of course, is the Treasury, if only because of Concorde's vast and to some, unexpected cost.

Among the projects studied by the Think Tank, which I am allowed to mention and on which we worked intensively, are Energy, the Shipbuilding Industry, the Coal Industry, Government Research & Development, the British Computer Industry, Public Expenditure, Nuclear Reactor Policy, Race Relations, Energy Conservation, Worker Participation, the UK Population, Electric Cars and, of course, the Government's Strategy, which more or less covers everything.

One of the rules I made at the start, nearly four years ago, was that we should not make reports or presentations unless they ended with precise recommendations for action. I did not think we were in business just to produce information.

My second, more difficult and more contentious rule was that when we produced reports, we should not bend over backwards to use the mellifluous style, if that is the right phrase, of the typical Civil Service report. (It is hardly necessary to say that there is no such thing as a typical Civil Service report – so large an organization is bound to produce both excellent writers of English and illiterates even in very high positions, because literacy is not, of course, an essential ingredient of being a top-class Civil Servant, *pace* Sir Ernest Gowers.) The result of this second rule has been, I hope, that our reports have erred on the side of directness if not brutality, and this has sometimes caused offence, as in the report on Government R & D which was published under my name even though a great deal of the work on it was done by another member of the Think Tank, while one chapter was virtually written by the Civil Service Department. Plain English, again *pace* Gowers, is neither particularly fashionable nor often appreciated; and it is frequently mistaken for rudeness.

My reference, a few minutes earlier, to the Civil Service Department prompts me to mention something which worries me about the Machinery of Government. I believe that in the Civil Service there is discrimination, very probably of a subconscious nature, against those with professional qualifications – I refer, for example, to scientists, engineers, accountants and lawyers. If you look at the qualifications of Senior Civil Servants, that is Permanent Secretaries, Deputy Secretaries and Under Secretaries, I think you will find that, using any yardstick, there are too few with professional qualifications. Even economists are treated as a separate species – hence the Government's Economic Service. I believe there is too much pedestalization of the 'generalist' or the so-called 'administrator' – too much fear of the technical world which, of course, the professional must be able to explain, with a few unimportant exceptions, in simple language. How many members of your profession are in the Civil Service on temporary secondment? One of the purposes of my report on Government R & D was to try, in the most modest of ways, to change this situation; and perhaps it had a very minor success in that, for example, the Ministry of Agriculture and the Department of Health now have Chief Scientists in relatively senior positions. But, no doubt by accident, when the terms of reference of Sir Hermann Bondi's task force were prepared, ostensibly to look into this subject, of the possibility of anti-professionalism to which I drew attention in my report, they did not deal with *it* but with an ancillary one, the mobility of scientists. That is an important, if intractable, question. But it is not the main point on my mind – the absence or paucity of good scientists or ex-scientists, engineers, accountants and even that currently despised class, businessmen, in the top corridors of Whitehall.

The six-monthly analyses of Government Strategy – I sometimes called them the headmaster's report – has not been possible under the present administration, perhaps because for the first three months the Government was believed to be wondering whether it would have a General Election in June and, for the next three, whether it would have one in the autumn. Such an atmosphere was not conducive to trying to answer the question 'Where are we going and why?' even if the effort would have been acceptable. As a matter of fact I have grave doubts about the 'Where are we going?' part of the question.

This brings me to one of the reasons why I asked the Prime Minister if he would release me from my duties this autumn, apart from being exhausted – because the job *has* been exhausting – and feeling pretty stale. The reason was that while trying to exercise a synoptic view of what I privately christened The Nation's Business, I became very worried; and I don't think someone who becomes very worried is the best person to run a Think Tank. The head of it should be abstracted from, though conscious of, the problems that caused that worry in me.

During the last four years I have become very conscious of the vast number of problems affecting this country about which I knew virtually nothing before and of which, I am ashamed to say, I was, in some cases, barely conscious. I refer, for example, to the following issues which are on my mind but not necessarily the subject, now or in the past, of the Think Tank's attention:

Is it really impossible to have a decent housing policy?

Should the Unions dictate the nation's social policy?

Is the current erosion of confidence in our economy justified?

How can the relationship between Government and the Nationalized Industries be improved? Or is everything all right?

Can one predict, in this country, the social and economic consequences of two consecutive years of inflation at more than 20% (if it occurs)?

Is a garbage man in Coventry or a Yorkshire miner interested in Giotto or the Duke of Devonshire's Florentine drawings?

Are letters out of date?

Is there a real danger of Fascism in Britain?

Should there be a minimum wage? Need it be so low as to be humiliating and derisory?

Should we be interested in airships?

To the extent it is now practised, is the level of secrecy which surrounds the operations of Government necessary?

Can we really not improve services for the elderly?

Should children be allowed to leave school before sixteen if they wish?

Is there enough fresh water in England, and will there be in ten years' time?

These questions, and the priorities to be assigned to them, are some that have come into my mind through beginning, vaguely, to understand some of the Nation's Business. They reflect a change in myself and the workings of my mind which used to be much more concerned with the conduct of research in general and research in reproductive physiology in particular. But, of course, it is too late for me to have a restless and enquiring mind. That is for people in their late twenties or early thirties, which is why I tried to recruit such people into the Think Tank. It was they who stimulated me to try and think, you may feel parochially, about the Nation's Business, some aspects of which I have briefly touched on this evening.

I hope you will not think from what I have just said, that I believe people are useless after the age of thirty-five; that they have nothing to contribute other than encourage the young, important as that is. So I will end with some remarks on this subject by Francis Bacon:

'Men of age object too much, consult too long, adventure too little, repent too soon, and seldom drive business home to the full period, but content themselves with a mediocrity of success. Young men, in the conduct and manage of actions, embrace more than they can hold; stir more than they can quiet; fly to the end, without consideration of the means and degrees; pursue some few principles which they have chanced upon absurdly; use extreme remedies at first; and, that which doubleth all errors, will not acknowledge or retract them; like an unready horse, that will neither stop nor turn.'

So perhaps a mixture, or should I say in this company an ecclesiastical egg, might be a useful compromise, if that is what we need to succeed in conducting the Nation's Business.

'By the way, whatever happened to the Think Tank?'

13
FAREWELL TO
THE THINK TANK

The Times, 13 October 1974

DEAR PRIME MINISTER,

From time to time I have had the privilege of reading the valedictory reports of Her Majesty's Ambassadors when retiring from their posts; and I have been greatly impressed by their mellifluous erudition. It would be useless for me to try to emulate their style; and, indeed, it might violate the principles of brevity (if not terseness) which, during nearly four years, I have tried to inculcate into your Central Policy Review Staff.

When the time came, as it now has, to look back on these years, I was deeply impressed first, at the many kindnesses I have received, both from politicians and officials; and secondly, at the number of subjects in which, to quote from an instruction by Sir Burke Trend, 'the CPRS has taken an interest'. Such diverse topics as energy, the British computer industry, counter-inflation, presenting information to ministers, nuclear reactors, race relations, regional policy, energy conservation, decision-making under stress, worker participation, UK population trends and coal have occupied the time of what Mr Len Murray once described to me as 'this amateur show'.

Nevertheless, there are several subjects in which I regret the Think Tank has not so far taken an interest: one of these is the effect of possible changes in our climate on the life of the inhabitants of this island. It would, I believe, repay study. Another is waste, by which I do not mean recycling, a subject which is being pursued so assiduously and indefatigably by Mr Oakes of the Department of the Environment. Finally, I wish we had had the time, the perseverance, or your instructions to set up a central but independent survey machine which, whatever anyone may say, does not exist, to help in finding out what the people really want Government policy to be on specific issues. (A survey machine is not, of course, referenda by another name.)

Politicians often believe that their world is the real one: officials sometimes take a different view. Having been a member of this latter and lesser breed, it is, perhaps, inevitable that I should have become increasingly fearful about the effects of the growing political hostility between and among our people. To what extent is this blinding us, preventing us keeping our eye on the real ball, assuming there is one? I think there is and I have said before what I believe *it* to be: that the people of Britain must now agree to the necessity for a period of national sacrifice, what the Governor of the Bank of England called austerity.

There is no chance of all of us maintaining our standard of living, of keeping up with inflation, even though politicians and other national leaders seem to think it axiomatic that this is both a possible and essential right of the people. We, the people, have no divine rights; only those that a democratic society can afford and has the will to provide. So if, in the interests of the future, democracy requires a freeze, rationing and harsh taxation of luxuries, it is no good saying that such measures are acceptable in war but not in peace: because we are at war, with ourselves and with that neo-Hitler, that arch enemy, inflation.

This is not to say that the underprivileged in our society – and I would not have Mr Jack Jones's temerity to define that phrase in quantitative terms – should remain in that condition. All the combined effort of which we are capable should be directed to shortening the time by when the word underprivileged will be insignificant on this island.

We shall never achieve this goal by divisive policies nor by ignoring the writing on the wall. It is, I think, clear how we could achieve it, given our acceptance of the unimportant hardships that are necessary.

It is customary nowadays to sneer at such concepts as the Dunkirk spirit, or the faith and courage of our nation when huge parts of London, Glasgow, Coventry and Plymouth were being destroyed. But the fact that we cannot point our finger at someone called Hitler, but only at something called inflation, does not make inflation and its evil consequences less dangerous than Hitler: more so in fact, because we have not – and no longer seem able to mobilize – the will to fight this new enemy with that formidable determination we exhibited in World War II and which won us the respect of the world.

Not all managers, farmers, trade unionists, politicians, miners, stockbrokers and, dare I say, peers are worthless, contemptible, disloyal, parasitic or perfect. Is there really no chance of them and all the others joining forces to fight the common enemy? Maybe coalitions or Governments of national unity are out of date and out of reality. Must that mean *no* national unity, *no* common cause, *no* understanding of that other person, *no* friendship? Because if it does, it also means no hope.

So, as by now you know, Prime Minister, I leave the arena troubled, anxious and not too hopeful; but still praying for understanding, cohesion and a new sense of national unity to defeat the most formidable enemies this country has so far encountered, inflation and social division.

Yours, etc,
ROTHSCHILD

14

TOO OLD?

The Melchett Lecture, 8 November 1972[18]

FIRST may I say how honoured I am both to receive the Melchett Medal and to have been invited to address you today. So distinguished and sophisticated an audience as that which faces me would deter the majority of speakers; but I have an additional reason for being nervous.

During the last year I have been variously described as speaking or writing with abrasive candour, as using irrelevant commercial terminology, but, at the same time, indulging in unintelligible Whitehall jargon. It seems that I am refreshing, though simultaneously managing to be perfunctory, unreadable, and to engage in pettifogging and linguistic points. What I say is too terse, poorly phrased and largely incomprehensible; but at the same time, according to one devoted ally, I write in pure Sir Ernest Gowers.

Hence my understandably nervous condition as I attempt to steer between the Scylla of Whitehall and the Charybdis of commerce, not to speak of circumventing the Palaeopolis of Academia. But I have two further problems. First, as a Civil Servant I am not supposed to talk about my work except in terms of excruciatingly boring generality. I had therefore to conceive a subject which has nothing to do with my 'Think Tank' and is not, so far as I know, a matter of current Government policy, though perhaps it should be. How it might be injected into the Whitehall machine with its interdepartmental committees is a matter on which one could speculate at considerable length; but not today. As Dr Kissinger has said: 'Committees are consumers and sometimes sterilizers of ideas, rarely creators of them.'

My second problem is equally simple. Not surprisingly, previous recipients of the Melchett Medal delivered their lectures on subjects relevant to the Institute of Fuel, for example:

Too Old?

My lips are temporarily, if somewhat indifferently, sealed on the last of these subjects; and I know little or nothing about power, energy or fuel. But even if my ignorance is profound about fuel *qua* fuel, I hope that the subject of my lecture may, nevertheless, provide *some* fuel for thought.

The thesis that I propound this evening is as follows: evidence drawn from a diversity of sources indicates that, in man, there is a distinct peak in many physical and mental capacities before the age of thirty, and a subsequent decline of these abilities with age. Our society, however, tends to make maximum use of these abilities many years after peak capacity. Should we not, therefore, take action to restructure opportunity in such a way as to tap more fully the greater abilities of the young? In short, are not most of us here this evening merely (or nearly) dinosaurs, clinging in ignorance to our patch of antediluvian sun? The paucity of direct research on this theme, whether pure or applied, if I dare use those adjectives, belies its importance. We live in a time of rapid technological and social change, and if we are to control and direct this change, and produce the innovations it makes necessary, then it is essential that we exploit to the full such human resources as are at our disposal. It may be that, by altering our systems of education and of vocational training and selection, we could make far better use of the peculiar abilities of the young than we do at present. But let me first present some of the evidence upon which this idea is based.

Studies of age-related changes in ability and performance consistently yield certain general points: first, those individuals who perform particularly well early in life tend to be the ones who deteriorate least with age.[24] Thus, the most excellent maintain a high standard to a late age. Secondly, variation in performance usually increases greatly with age, so that the performance of any individual becomes harder to predict as he grows older. Thirdly, for those abilities that show a peak performance at a certain age, the age range for best performance is much narrower for the most excellent individuals than it is for the rest, so that the peak years for the *best* poets, athletes and thinkers fall between pretty narrow limits. Let me add, parenthetically, that purported counter-examples to this thesis tend to be in fact concealed instances of the first of these three generalizations; if you object that Smith is doing brilliant work at the age of seventy-five, then I would ask you to consider what genius he might have shown if he had had that opportunity at twenty-five. When Dean Swift, as an old man, re-read his Tale of a Tub, which he had written when quite young, he said 'Good God, what a genius I had when I wrote that book!' But, he had recently finished Gulliver's Travels.

The purely physical situation has also been epitomized by Welford,[24] who said: 'The successive changes of bodily, including neural, structure which take place between birth and old age are clearly such that, if the human organism is viewed as a piece of anatomical and physiological machinery, it rises to a peak of efficiency in the early twenties, and thereafter slowly declines.'

Physical strength falls into this pattern. It has been shown that maximum grip strength, and grip strength over a period of time, are both at their peak in the early twenties.[25,26] As early as 1884, Francis Galton showed that strength of pull and swiftness of blow are at a maximum at about twenty-five. Speed of movement is at its greatest in the late teens. It is no coincidence that there have been very young athletes of great excellence; one thinks of Shane Gould, of Evonne Goolagong, of Little Mo and of many others. There are of course certain sports, such as riding, bowling and billiards, in which experience is at a greater premium than physical efficiency, but in all those sports which require speed or strength, the excellence of youth is at once apparent. And the clarity with which this age pattern is to be observed in sport is due precisely to its essentially meritocratic nature; there is very little bias of opportunity in favour of a particular age group in sport. Indeed it is one of the few areas of human enterprise in which youth is not actively foiled.

'What, then', you may ask, appalled at this vision of brute physical efficiency, 'of David and Goliath? Is not intelligence the master of strength?' Alas, there is abundant evidence that David's intellectual mastery of the situation could well have been connected with his youth, even if he was helped by Goliath's possible pituitary problems.

Brain weight peaks at about twenty-five, and the number of cortical cells, after a period of constancy from birth to the early twenties, declines sharply to the nineties.[27] Each day of our adult lives more than 100,000 nerve cells die and nerve cells are never, of course, replaced. In spite of one specious or even, perhaps, facetious assertion that this loss is associated with increased memory storage,[28] it seems far more plausible to associate such physiological decay with the less pleasant aspects of ageing, with decreased learning ability, shorter memory span, and lower non-verbal IQ.

Experimental psychology provides a wealth of similar evidence. Reaction time to a stimulus peaks in the early twenties, speed of movement in the late teens. In tests requiring fast and complex sequential movements older subjects can maintain the speed of the young only at the expense of accuracy. This is because in older subjects a limitation in the capacity of central processes necessitates a longer time to initiate, guide and monitor movements. Given a choice, older subjects will always tend to shift the balance between speed and accuracy towards the latter. Older subjects are further hampered by difficulty in making decisions while executing movements which means that, after the twenties, people have increasing difficulty in executing paced tasks requiring the employment of more than one faculty. Such tasks should, therefore, be given chiefly to younger workers. Complex substitution and hand-to-eye coordination also show peak performance in the early twenties, as do writing speed and the ability to synthesize data to form an integrated whole, to identify new objects, to process complex information and to solve problems. This seems in part due to a short-term memory deficiency that makes it hard for older subjects simultaneously to retain many pieces of information. Long-term memory is unaffected by age, which is consistent with the evident ability of many older people to use experience in forming judgements.[24] But performance in learning tasks and the ability to think critically and evaluate evidence both decline from a peak in the early twenties.[29] Performance in many IQ tests shows a similar pattern[30] and, however beset with difficulties of interpretation, some IQ tests are still the best measure we have of adult intelligence. A limited analysis is not necessarily a faulty one.

As in the experimental sphere, so too in everyday life: research on age and performance carried out in society, rather than in the laboratory, yields results in keeping with my thesis. The most outstanding work in chemistry, for example, is usually done in the late thirties; mathematicians, physicists, inventors, doctors, philosophers, sculptors and writers very often do their best work in their thirties. However, I believe that these results reflect a combination of the social opportunity-structure and the lengthy training period deemed necessary in our educational system; for there is much evidence to suggest that if gifted individuals are allowed to perform early, they do so and their work is frequently outstanding. Thus, most outstanding poetry is written before the age of thirty. Marconi made his main discovery at the age of twenty-two. Michaelangelo was famous throughout Europe in his twenties, Jenner made his discovery very young. Mozart started composing as a child and, through his father's influence, the younger Pitt could show his ability to lead the country at the age of twenty-four. Schubert, Galileo, Blake, Bizet, Burns, Joule, Keats, Milton, Pascal, Pope, Rossini, Shelley and Tolstoy were all doing creative work before the age of twenty-one, and Newton, Dirac, Maxwell (while an undergraduate) and Fraunhofer were also very early starters.

Early opportunity evidently fosters excellence; thus many first-class golfers have lived near a golf course from early youth, and most outstanding musicians first showed promise and started to train before the age of seven.

Youth has proved itself in the military sphere. Alexander the Great led a decisive cavalry charge at the age of eighteen, Hannibal invaded Italy at the age of twenty-nine, Don John of Austria commanded victoriously against the Turks at Lepanto when only twenty-six. In 1346 the Black Prince became a first-class commander at eighteen. In the Thirty Years' War, the conscripted Swedes who fought so well for France were all under thirty. In the conquest of Canada Wolfe was given command at thirty-two, largely through Pitt's refusal to let the jealousies of senior officers prevent his advance. To a Minister complaining bitterly of the appointment of 'this madman Wolfe', George II was heard to bark 'Mad is he? I wish to heavens he would bite some of my other generals!' Napoleon received command of the French armies in Italy at the age of twenty-six, and Nelson was made a post-captain at twenty. In more modern terms, the performance of the Israeli generals, almost all under forty, in the Six Day War compares favourably with that of the venerable British High Command in World War I. And then there was that Mogul general in the sixteenth century, Babur, aged fourteen, leading his army to victory by day and, at night, weeping in his tent for his absent mother.

Of course there are numerous cases anomalous to my thesis – Grandma Moses and Cervantes come to mind – but half-an-hour spent leafing through a dictionary of biography will provide legion examples favourable to my view. Furthermore, let me emphasize once again that high performance late in life serves to confute my thesis only if it can be shown that, in spite of opportunity, the individual in question was positively unsuccessful in the enterprises of his youth.

In sum, then, it appears that much of the significant record of the human race has been made by men and women scarcely older than the hundreds of thousands of students who mill like lemmings in our schools and universities.

That matters should be as I hope by now to have persuaded you they are, is, in biological terms, hardly surprising. It is only with the recent development of effective medicine that the average life span has been extended much beyond the thirties, and it may well be that physically and psychologically, man is still adapted to a short life, with peak prowess in the late teens and twenties. And at a recent meeting of the European Cell Biology Organization, it seemed generally agreed that we neither understand the phenomenon of ageing, nor have we the ability to prevent it. Is it not therefore reasonable that we should seek to tap human ability at its peak, rather than assume in feeble optimism that we will find a way to prevent or delay our all too hasty deterioration?

In fact, our society is one of massive human waste, youth being denied opportunity at every turn. Lehman[31], for instance, has collected much detailed information which shows that American Presidents, British Cabinet Ministers, Presidents of Republics,

Ambassadors, military leaders, judges, Presidents of Learned Societies, financiers, bankers, lawyers, senior doctors, psychologists, chemists, heads of educational institutions, leaders in commerce and industry, Popes and Bishops, are, virtually without exception, over the age of fifty. Indeed, religion, it is interesting to note, presents a clear paradigm: the founders of new religions, Christ for example, tend to be young, usually in their early thirties. But while it is men in their prime who conceive the great religions, it is the old who make them prevail, so that instituted and dogmatic religion owes its existence chiefly to men well advanced in years.

We may, I hope, take it that election to the Royal Society is a mark of achievement. But even here, as A. V. Hill has shown, there is a distinct bias against youth. Hill[32-34] found that for the years 1848–1960 the median age differed according to subject, falling in the early forties or late thirties for mathematics and physics, and in the middle fifties for engineering and geology. Thus the age of election tends to be considerably greater than the age of maximum ability discussed earlier. Hill himself points out that: 'A median age of forty-eight and a half at election, although young compared with that of many academics, is old compared with the age at which high scientific merit can generally be recognized with certainty.' And election to the Royal Society is not supposed to be just a prize for services rendered, but also an appointment to a living, working community with a function towards Science and the State. In Hill's own words, 'There is no doubt that a Fellow can take his part in it better if he is elected young . . . academies can be ruined by electing people too old!' On the 1st August of this year, 1972, the average age of the Royal Society Fellows was no less than sixty-three. One cannot, of course, stop people getting older; and retirement at sixty, as in the Civil Service, would not be appropriate. But a two-tier system, a subject to which I shall revert later, could, perhaps, be studied with advantage.

Maximum income, too, shows a peak at a late age – the middle fifties, which I suspect is socially and economically wrong. But it will be a formidable task to change the upward drift of incomes, or even the shape of the curve.

Collectively, then, these data suggest that authority, prestige and responsibility tend to gravitate to elderly men, past the peak of their physical and psychological capabilities. There are several possible explanations for this.

Success is largely a social phenomenon. Nepotism, luck, inheritance, able subordinates and collaborators, and a vast complex of other factors determine success, and the manipulation or allotment of such factors may depend on abilities and circumstances quite unrelated to the sheer organic capacity to perform well. Now it may be neither possible nor desirable to interfere with this situation, except in the broadest possible way, by providing increased opportunity for young people to reach senior positions, but it seems to me that both reason and necessity compel us to this latter attempt.

A second reason for this state of affairs is that early performance may ensure success in fields to which the early talents are quite irrelevant. Thus we have Ronald Reagan and Shirley Temple, both of whom used their early popularity as actors as, apparently, their sole qualification successfully to enter politics. Granted, England is not yet California, but we are all familiar with the uncomfortable spectacle of the scientist who produces one outstanding paper at an early age, is elected to a Chair and subsequently produces nothing of any great value. In other words, early success may confer an accolade which turns out to be quite undeserved in later life.

Hall[35] has suggested another reason for the predominance of the old. He points out that those ageing individuals who have felt their powers beginning to wane, at least the more sagacious of them, have invented or adopted numerous devices whereby they safeguard their persons, goods and prestige. Thus, as a young man senesces, he takes continuous action to maintain his position. Certainly there are said to be many bureaucrats whose sole job is the preservation of their office. And if you find Hall's suggestion unrealistically Machiavellian, I would ask you to consider a common phenomenon: age tends to bring with it an impression of improvement; as one gets older, one tends to think one gets better at whatever one does, with certain obvious exceptions of an athletic nature, using this phrase in the broadest sense. Now, while in many cases this impression may be justified, it seems at least good, conservative reason to reflect that after all, if you are going ga-ga, you may already be so ga-ga that you fail to notice your own condition. And I trust that I have already shown without doubt that, at least in physiological terms, gagadom sets in early.

One ominous point here is that the usual age of leadership in various fields appears to have increased since the eighteenth century, and this seems to be a real trend, not to be explained away in terms of reduced mortality. And it seems also that the age for creative work is becoming lower. Thus the gap between the age of maximum usefulness, and that at which maximum use is made, is actually widening rather than shrinking as one might hope.

At this point, before I consider what might in practice be done to rectify this gap, let me make a brief disclaimer: it has not been my intention to suggest that intelligence *tout court* wanes with age. Such a suggestion would be both methodologically foolish in the face of our lack of any hard, scientific standard by which intelligence may accurately be measured, and also plainly untrue, when one remembers our readiness to accept as the operations of intelligence many abilities in which experience plays an undoubted part. Clearly there exists a balance in judgement between experience and organic efficiency. For certain tasks experience is at a greater premium than is speedy and ruthless logic. Politics is or may be a case in point, while for others the reverse is true. I am not, therefore, advocating a complete hand-over to youth of the social reins. But, while intelligence may be seasoned to advantage by a certain amount of experience, it remains true that what does wane in man, and that quite early in life, is creativity, that mysterious serendipity in the formation of hypotheses and the connexion of seemingly unrelated data without which all of our greatest, and many of our more trivial, achievements would not have been made. Thus we might do well to make increased use of young people in senior positions even in such experience-based areas as politics, industry and administration. There is an obvious and conservative criterion for the extent of this use of the young, based on the fact that the actual performance of an individual in society is not always limited by his capacity. Clearly a pen-pushing worker needs no great strength. The occupations in which young workers could be especially useful are those requiring physical strength, e.g. labouring jobs, those requiring rapid reflexes and good hand-to-eye co-ordination, for example, surgery, certain factory work, precision scientific work and so on (but not driving cars because the young have about four times as many accidents as the old and middle-aged); and those occupations requiring the ability to learn quickly and apply new ideas to new situations and co-ordinate large amounts of information, for example in industry, politics, the professions and education. As with all strong medicines, youth should be used no more than is necessary.

Now one might object that, if we are to grant to creative youth initiative, leaving to the old the administration for which their brains and experience are so well suited, then even with all the goodwill in the world, the bureaucratic dinosaurism that is already so conspicuous in society cannot fail to get worse. On the face of it, this seems a real dilemma: if administration is already two steps behind the ideas and plans of those who initiate change and if, therefore, you hand over the initiative function to a less conservative group, the administrators will be thoroughly outpaced. And to resolve this conflict by employing the most creative people as bureaucrats is to commit exactly the waste one is trying to avoid. But it seems to me that this apparent dilemma is a virtue in disguise, serving at once both to keep the bureaucrats up to scratch, and to bridle the inexperienced impetuosity of youth. Indeed, one might envisage a more or less formally instituted two-tier system in which youth would be granted more power for initiative than it has at present, while age held fairly strong powers of delay and, I suppose, the periodic application of accumulated wisdom. Such a two-tier system is not unknown in industry, for example in Germany and the Netherlands.

The average age of those cardinals of bureaucracy in the United Kingdom, the Permanent Secretaries, is, including your lecturer, fifty-seven, beating the Royal Society by no less than six years. But they have to go earlier, at sixty, apart from a few unimportant exceptions.

'But why, then,' you might further object, 'if the old are indeed over-utilized at the expense of their juniors, why do we not, when a man or woman reaches fifty or sixty, simply apply that Gordian recipe of Queen Elizabeth the First to Cecil (in another context), "Get out!": in other words, earlier retirement?' Now, while this might have a beneficial effect on the unemployment figures, and I repeat *figures*, and while, as I hope by now is clear, I am far from thinking that people should go on doing the same job from the cradle to the grave, yet it seems to me that earlier retirement is not the correct solution; for citizens who work contribute to the country's total wealth whereas those who live on transfer payments do not. Like the unemployed, the retired belong to this latter category. But they differ from the unemployed in that they rarely go back to work when the economy re-expands. At a given level of population, therefore, the more citizens who are retired, the lower the country's productive potential, and, assuming one believes in growth, the lower its underlying capacity for growth.

The only valid defence of early retirement would be that high unemployment is otherwise incurable. And if this doctrine of despair were really true, then faster emigration might be a better long-term treatment for structural unemployment.

To return, then, to my thesis, it is obvious that increased opportunity for young hopefuls depends greatly on the goodwill of the older men who at present have control. Given this and to make an optimist's assumption, a first step towards making the young available when they are most useful would be to change the structure of education. Education has in recent years become something of a sacred cow, in that any public discussion of the subject is constrained to pay lip-service to an egalitarian fetichism that holds as taboo and not-to-be-tampered-with certain absolutes like the Right of Education and the School Leaving Age (which I believe we should lower, if we can change the style and aims of formal education). As with all taboo objects, even to talk about these principles in any but the most conservative terms is to place oneself in great danger. It is ironic that the cause of such superstition is the perfectly correct realization that education is, perhaps, the only possible avenue to a solution of our present social malaise, while that malaise itself has engendered a set of values that makes the *particular* changes required in our education system well-nigh impossible, if only for political reasons. But even if the changes I am about to suggest strike you as being as monstrous as a repeal of the Factories' Acts, let us be quite clear that, as it now stands, our educational system is a cumbrous and obsolete beast, ripe for the knife.

It has been thought in the past that certain things cannot be taught to children below the age of eight since they lack the ability to make logically transitive inferences, an idea largely due to Piaget.[36] Recent work at Oxford,[37] however, suggests that certain basic skills such as measurement and counting and, I suspect, reading, writing and languages, can be taught to children from a very early age, much earlier than they are at present. We could therefore cease formal school training earlier, and perhaps leave university training until thirty or later except for those who wish to pursue academic careers or become teachers. The University of the Air shows how this can be achieved, even in the home, and a microscopic number of industrialists are getting confirmation on the shop floor.

Evidence suggests that performance at the University is unaffected by age. Moreover, our present educational system is grossly inefficient even in its own terms; the advent of computers on a large scale, and the concomitant easy and swift retrieval of information, has rendered our schools' continuing insistence on rote-learning quite anachronistic. Churchill was often bottom of his form at Harrow; but Harrow, like virtually all schools then and now, tested its inmates for anything or, perhaps, everything other than creativity. It could be said that our present examination-ridden system measures the size of a student's *gluteus maximus* rather than that of his mind, and is quite unfit to develop individual talent. With ready access to a wide range of information, all the modern schoolchild need be taught is method, how to find the information he needs to work with, and no doubt a modicum of basic factual and operational information. Memory is no longer at a premium. Much of the dislike of school would vanish if such a new system were developed and the old order relegated to the ashcan. Such a system would to some extent do away with the evils of specialization. It is thought at present that specialization is a necessary evil, since learning has become so large that no one individual can possibly have a thorough knowledge of more than a very small field of study. Such an attitude ignores the fact that, in many fields of study or endeavour, a complete knowledge of the field is unnecessary, provided that the student can quickly gain such knowledge when and if he needs it. With instant access to any information, the pupil would be freed to develop a far more widely ranging set of interests than it is possible for him to pursue at present. This would doubtless both liberate the creativity that contemporary education so successfully suppresses, and, as a spin-off, provide a partial answer to the problem that increasing leisure has raised. With a wide range of interests developed from early youth, the distinction between work and leisure would be less sharp and obvious.

Maybe we have something to learn from the emphasis placed on co-operation between pupils in China. A co-operative approach to education could be combined with a system of apprenticeship to learn basic skills or factual information necessary for any particular work and, by means of early assessment of their skills, children could be channelled into appropriate training programmes.

This latter notion is not, of course, without its dangers. Many people would assert that to insist on an individual being used by society to do what he is best at, when he is best at it, would be a serious infringement of individual freedom. Many, particularly among the young, also feel that everyone has the right, as an individual, to make no contribution to society at all, if that is what he desires, and any procedure for channelling children into one kind of training or another would therefore have to be handled with great care. But I am convinced that the speeding-up of early education, combined with the breadth of learning made possible by computerized information and teaching systems, would be as beneficial to the individuals as it is necessary for society.

In partial summary, then, I quote Professor J. Z. Young:[38]

'As we grow older . . . the brain ceases to profit from experiment, it becomes set into patterns of laws. The well-established laws of a well-trained person may continue to be usefully applied to situations already experienced, though they fail to meet new ones. Here we see with startling clearness the basis of some of the most familiar features of human society, the adventure, subversiveness, inventiveness and resource of the young; the informed and responsible wisdom of the old. At each stage of the development of our brains, we have a special contribution to make.'

Or perhaps, more succinctly, the old French proverb:

> '*Si jeunesse savait,*
> *Si vieillesse pouvait.*'

15

LORD ROSEBERY
1882-1974

Memorial Service at the Guards Chapel,
3 July 1974

So much has been said in the Press about Harry Rosebery's prowess in all forms of sport – cricket, racing, shooting, racquets, golf (at which he was as difficult to beat as he was in argument), and hunting; about his uncanny gift with animals, including in recent years his beloved parrot Inky; about his extraordinary success with Allenby; about him as Regional Commissioner for Scotland – that it would weary you if I were, once again, to recount his many triumphs – or single out one particular innings or one particular race. Nor do I propose to dwell on his marvellous family home, Dalmeny, with its black-faced sheep mowing the lawns; and with the best claret cellar in the United Kingdom including what *was* a famous tappit hen. Instead I would like to dwell very briefly on the other man, known to some, but not, perhaps, to all of you.

In Harry Rosebery's Obituary in *The Times* he was described as a 'blunt and straightforward personality'. Neither of these attributes is enough to describe the man. His bluntness was turned on and off at will, often with considerable effect. Anyone who saw him with young people, with whom, unlike many of the older generation, he had a remarkable knack of getting on – of establishing a rapport – realized that he knew the virtues of silence, of understatement and of the sympathetic listener. Nor was his personality in any way straightforward, whatever he chose to let some, or indeed many, people think. He had a subtle mind, an almost feminine intuition and great speed of thought, so that the well-known blunt manner took in many people.

Harry Rosebery had the Midas touch, whether it was to do with the Derby winner, business (to which I shall revert later), or breeding a champion ram. He knew three years ahead what shape of animal Smithfield would want. He was never tired, because of his fantastic energy; he was interested in and curious about everything, down to the minutest detail. These character-istics combined with a marvellous memory and some sort of computer in his brain, enabled him to sift, analyse and digest information at a speed which made his opinions *seem* intuitive. He did not understand his own ability to store and synthesize facts and impressions, and draw the correct inferences from them; but among other things it made him an excellent judge of character. This he coupled with the ability to form personal relationships equally with soldiers, stockmen, the young and the very young, financiers, policemen, politicians and *even* his relatives like me.

At the end of World War I when my family Bank was still a Partnership and you could not be a Partner unless called Roths-child, my father, who was then in charge, used to say 'There is only one non-Rothschild I would really like to be a Partner. It is, of course, Harry.' My father, who was a shy, introverted character, would not have said this about a 'blunt and straightforward personality'.

We are in this great Chapel which literally rose, phoenix-like, out of the ashes of senseless destruction, to honour and pay tribute to the memory of a man who, even in the last months of his life – I spent some time with him three weeks before he died – looked to the future with hope and optimism. He was making plans for his Golden Wedding which would have taken place a few days ago. It is therefore fitting that I should end with a quotation appropriate to him and to the place in which we honour his memory. It was said in 1940.

'Goodnight, then; sleep to *gather* strength for the morning, for the morning will come. Brightly will it shine on the brave and true, the kindly, and all who suffer for the cause, and gloriously upon the tombs of heroes. Thus will shine the dawn.'

16

NEED FOR A FARMING POLICY NOT A POLITICAL FOOTBALL

The Times, 15 November 1974

In *The Times* of October 1, I expressed anxiety about the 'growing political hostility between and among our people'. Since then I have been told on several occasions how naive it was to expect opposing political parties not to oppose each other. 'The duty of an opposition is to oppose', as Lord Randolph Churchill said, as if we did not all know by now. That is not at all what I was referring to. In this article I give one example of what *was* on my mind – British agriculture, which should be extra-political, but is not.

Anyone deeply involved during the winter of 1973 in the oil crisis will not wish to go through that ordeal again. Memories are conveniently short; so it is worth mentioning that not only were our oil supplies reduced, but also there was a constant fear or threat, it does not matter which, that oil might actually be cut off.

After energy, or before it for that matter, what is the greatest threat to this country? How can we most easily and quickly be paralysed? The answer is very obvious: food, or to be precise, lack of it. We have to eat to live and work. Without food it does not matter whether oil is cut off or not and the same applies, albeit to a lesser extent, if we have to pay blackmail prices for our imported food, which in 1973 cost no less than £2534m (excluding drink), 47% of what we needed and 17% of our total import bill.

As everyone knows, the policy of importing so much food was to a considerable extent predicated on the availability of cheaper food elsewhere than at home. That is no longer true and never will be again, first, because there are no countries left whose food production can be exploited (as the oil producing countries were); secondly, because world living standards, including food consumption, are increasing in spite of horror regions such as Bengal, Bangladesh and parts of Central Africa such as Mauritania, Mali, Niger and Chad; and thirdly, because world food consumption – and therefore food prices – will increase inexorably with world population. Because of these factors, there will not, in future, be any major food surpluses.

Given these facts and inferences from them, and I do not believe any logical person without an axe to grind could dispute them, it is depressing to read a paper, published in April, 1974, by the Trade Union Research Unit at Ruskin College, Oxford. It was called *Farm Incomes: the Separation of Reality from Illusion.* It is hard to believe that so prestigious an organization could have agreed inadvertently to the publication of biased data. What then was the axe to be ground (or wielded) which triumphed over logic? I believe there were two: first, a counterblast to the warnings about the state of British agriculture uttered by the National Farmers' Union (NFU), warnings, incidentally, which have now been fully justified by the unparalleled slaughtering by British farmers of pigs, cows, calves and poultry. But why is a counterblast needed? Surely the Trade Union Unit cannot object to the NFU lobbying on behalf of British farmers. After all, that is what union leaders do all the time on behalf of their members and, from time to time, for other causes; and very successful they are at it, too.

The second reason for the Trade Union Unit's distortion of the facts is, I believe, dislike of the farming community, something that is shared by many urban dwellers to a greater or lesser extent. What is the cause of this emotion? The answer can only be the sixth deadly sin. In recent years agriculture has been one of the most efficient British industries in spite of a constantly falling labour force and a major reduction in land available for agriculture, 60,000 acres per year. Even with these difficulties, output per head from 1964–73 grew more in agriculture (60%) than in manufacturing industries (49%), mining and quarrying (33%), metal manufacture (27%), vehicles (30%) or all production industries (49%).

The distortions in the Trade Union Unit's paper are as follows:

—The examination of changes in farm income starts from the year 1968, which was a notoriously bad harvest year for many farmers. This selection obviously accentuates the subsequent rise in farm incomes. Actually, the national net income from farming was about £50 million below the 'normal weather' estimate for 1968, and the average full-time net income was at its lowest since 1963.

—The paper contains a graph purporting to show the annual trend in farm incomes; but it has been restricted to the period 1948–68, subsequent figures being ignored. This makes the slope of the paper's farm income trend line artificially low. (Incidentally, the wrong sort of trend line, a straight one, was used, whereas a concave one would have been more appropriate.)

—The paper makes no reference to the fact that agriculture is about 80% financed by individual farmers and land owners and that retained farm earnings are therefore the biggest single source of money for annual investment in farming; nor does it say anything about the increase there has been in such investment since 1968. The increase has in fact been 60%.

—There is no reference to the large element in net farm income represented by valuation increases.

—There is no reference to the effects of inflation on money incomes and none, therefore, to the trend in farm income in real terms.

—There is no reference to the unprecedented increases in incomes in other sectors of the economy in recent years.

—There is no reference to the direct or indirect support given by Government to other industries to maintain income or profit.

—There is no reference to the import savings achieved by increased home food production.

—The paper refers critically to 'a diversion of an extra share of the nation's resources into' agriculture. This emotive statement is made without factual support or any comment on the merits of resources used in agriculture. In fact, exchequer support for agriculture declined sharply, both in real terms and per unit of output, from 1967 to 1972. Furthermore, the Central Statistical

Office's publications on capital formation in agriculture in comparison with the rest of the economy certainly do not support the suggestion of 'diversion'.

Although I believe it important to dispose, as a matter of principle, of false propaganda, there are more important things on the agenda to do with British farming, the most obvious of which are: How can this country make itself more immune to troubles or even crises of the winter-1973 type mentioned earlier? What should we grow? What more should we grow? What will happen to British farming and food prices if Mr Bottini's proposal for a £38 per week minimum agricultural wage is implemented? How can we stop 60,000 acres of agricultural land disappearing each year? How much will home food production decrease if there is a wealth tax on agricultural land in an industry financed almost entirely by individuals and not shareholders as in most other industries? These are questions which must be ventilated and discussed.

The nation's food should not and need not be a political football, if only because neither of the main parties has much to crow about on this front, leaving aside some election promises. So why not formulate an agricultural policy, setting the guidelines for the next ten years? Why not praise the farmers for the excellent job they have done?

17

ARE YOU FIT TO MAKE DECISIONS AFTER A LONG AIR FLIGHT AND TWO EXTRA GINS?

The Times, 24 December 1974

WHEN I was head of the Government's Think Tank the powers that be – it would, of course, be a breach of the Official Secrets Act to mention them by name – allowed me to spend a little of my time on private activities of an entrepreneurial nature. These were not, I hasten to say, of the financial sort – that would have been a breach of Estacode, the Civil Service's *n* commandments – just initiative of a personal as opposed to the Think Tank sort. This article is concerned with one of these initiatives, termed, for the benefit of Whitehall, Decision Making under Stress.

You do not need someone who, until recently, was an official (or civil servant, as they are often called), and who was paid *inter alia* (see frontispiece) to observe the behaviour of ministers, to tell you that Cabinet ministers, trade union leaders, business tycoons, senior civil servants (or officials as they are often called), financiers and generals, admirals and air-marshals, not to speak of field-marshals, often have to take very important decisions, sometimes soon after a long flight, over-indulgence the evening before or even the same day (those lunches), or when one has, simply, been overdoing it and could do with a day or so off.

It is, of course, very difficult for extremely busy and important people to pause and ask themselves such questions as: 'Am I in a fit condition to take a decision in two hours' time?', 'Will I be able to follow my colleagues' reasoning at Cabinet later this morning?'; and some extremely busy and important people do not even like the idea that their powers of logical reasoning or their judgement could be a little below par. (The word par, as I shall show, is important, even though no competitions are involved in what follows, except with oneself.) 'Ill effects of a transatlantic flight or those extra gin and tonics yesterday evening? Nonsense, I can adjust to such situations; so straight into the meeting'. But can you? Do you? Of course, you do not want to subject yourself to examination by someone else and conceivably undergo the risk or – dare I say it – the humiliation of being found to be below par. From now on that is quite unnecessary because *The Times* provides you today with a secret and personal do-it-yourself kit, so that in future no one need ever know why you had that meeting, or your contribution to it, deferred.

The test at the end of this article (invented by A. D. Baddeley of the Medical Research Council) contains a number of short sentences, each followed by a pair of letters, AB or BA. The sentences claim to describe the order of the two letters, that is to say which comes first. They can do this in several different ways. Thus the order AB can be correctly described by saying either:

  (i) A precedes B, or
 (ii) B follows A, or
(iii) B does not precede A, or
(iv) A does not follow B.

These are correct descriptions of the pair AB but not if applied to the other pair, BA.

If you decide to test your state of mind, read each sentence 1–64 in the table on page 147 and decide whether it is a true or false description of the letter pair which follows it. If you think the sentence describes the letter pair correctly, put a tick in the first column headed 'True'. If you think the sentence does not give you a true description of the letter order, put a tick in the second column headed 'False'.

This is illustrated in examples (i) and (ii) below. Having read (i) and (ii), try examples (iii) to (vi):

	True	*False*
(i) A follows B – BA	✔	
(ii) B precedes A – AB		✔
(iii) A is followed by B – AB		
(iv) B is not followed by A – BA		
(v) B is preceded by A – BA		
(vi) A does not precede B – BA		

When you start the main test, work as quickly as you can without making mistakes. You may well be able to finish the test in three minutes but whether you can or not, do *not* spend more than three minutes on it. (No kudos attaches to answering all the questions because you are only concerned with your own performance on different occasions.) Start with sentence 1 and work systematically through the test, leaving no blank spaces. Compare your marks at various times of the day or night, and on different occasions such as after a particularly busy week, a holiday, a long air trip, etc.

You would be well advised to do five exploratory runs during one or two weeks to get over the brief 'learning period', that is improvement with practice.

It is important to remember that you are not competing with anyone else in this exercise: nor is it an intelligence test in which a high score could occasion satisfaction. You now have a do-it-yourself kit with which you can examine your powers of logical reasoning or state of mind under varying environmental conditions. Even if the types of question you have to ask yourself – and answer correctly – are of a different nature, e.g. have all the relevant factors been taken into consideration, a satisfactory score in the AB – BA test means that you are in good shape to deal with your particular problem and *vice versa*.

Did I hear you say 'What happened when you tried it on ministers and senior civil servants?'? I am, of course, forbidden to answer that question: but I am allowed to say that a few in both classes agreed to be guinea-pigs but, as the test requires, they kept the results to themselves.

The correct answers to questions 1–64 on the next page are on page 180.

Are you fit to make decisions?

ANSWER AS MANY ITEMS AS YOU CAN IN 3 MINUTES

Item	True	False	Item	True	False
1. A is preceded by B – BA	✓		33. A does not follow B – AB	✓	
2. A is not followed by B – BA		✓	34. A is not followed by B – BA	✓	
3. B is preceded by A – BA		✓	35. B follows A – BA	✓	
4. A is followed by B – AB	✓		36. B is not preceded by A – BA	✓	
5. A does not follow B – AB		✓	37. B is preceded by A – BA		✓
6. B is not preceded by A – AB		✓	38. A is not preceded by B – BA		✓
7. B follows A – AB		✓	39. B precedes A – BA	✓	✓
8. A precedes B – BA		✓	40. B follows A – BA		✓
9. B does not follow A – BA		✓	41. B is followed by A – BA	✓	
10. B precedes A – AB		✓	42. A follows B – AB		✓
11. B is followed by A – BA			43. B does not precede A – BA		✓
12. B is not followed by A – BA		✓	44. A does not precede B – BA	✓	
13. B is preceded by A – AB	✓	✓	45. A is preceded by B – BA	✓	
14. B is followed by A – AB	✓		46. B is not followed by A – AB	✓	
15. B precedes A – BA	✓		47. A precedes B – BA		✓
16. A is not followed by B – AB	✓		48. B does not follow A – BA		
17. A is followed by B – BA	✓		49. A is followed by B – AB	✓	
18. B is not preceded by A – BA		✓	50. B is not preceded by A – AB		✓
19. B is followed by A – AB	✓		51. A does not precede B – AB		✓
20. A does not follow B – BA		✓	52. A follows B – BA	✓	✓
21. B does not precede A – AB	✓		53. A is not followed by B – AB		✓
22. A is preceded by B – AB	✓		54. A is not preceded by B – AB	✓	✓
23. B is not followed by A – AB		✓	55. A does not follow B – BA		✓
24. A is not preceded by B – BA		✓	56. A is followed by B – BA	✓	✓
25. A follows B – BA	✓		57. B does not follow A – AB		✓
26. A is not preceded by B – AB		✓	58. B does not precede A – AB	✓	
27. A follows B – AB		✓	59. B is not followed by A – BA		✓
28. A does not precede B – AB		✓	60. B does not follow A – AB		✓
29. A precedes B – AB	✓		61. A precedes B – AB	✓	
30. B is preceded by A – AB	✓		62. A is preceded by B – AB		✓
31. B does not precede A – BA		✓	63. B precedes A – AB		✓
32. A does not precede B – BA	✓		64. B follows A – AB	✓	

147

18

NUCLEAR POWER FOR
GOOD OR EVIL?

'I think the future will (not) *look after the future'*
The Times, 27 September 1976

There were some punctuation errors and one mistake in this article. They have been corrected in this version.

The Flowers Report, the main subject of this article, has been quite severely criticized and it follows that my article is liable to some of the same criticisms. Nevertheless, one of the most eminent critics of the Flowers Report, Lord Hinton, had this to say in the House of Lords (Hansard, 1977, column 1349):

'The Commission is right in criticizing atomic energy organizations for being dilatory in devising safe methods for disposing of fission products.'

*

THERE is an after-supper game which can be quite thought-provoking: listing those people who have most changed the world. Jesus, Lenin and Plato come to mind; and a number of others such as St Paul, Marx, Newton, Moses, Darwin, Muhammad, Confucius and Mao Tse-tung. Others will doubtless think of others.

Today, it is, perhaps, unlikely that someone of the stature of those mentioned above will appear. We are in an age of committees, councils, commissions, working parties, task forces and panels. But there are precedents for such organizations having a major effect on the future of the world: the Council of Nicaea initiated a Creed which influenced the Christian world up to the present time. *Nuclear Power and the Environment,* the sixth report of the Royal Commission on Environmental Pollution – Chairman Sir Brian Flowers – could influence the world and its mainly helpless inhabitants for as long as anyone may care to conceive: among other matters mentioned later, *Nuclear Power and the Environment* deals with the deliberate accumulation – on our earth, by its inhabitants – of some of the most deadly substances known, when it is at any rate questionable whether it is necessary to do so in conditions of incomplete safety.

Moreover, the accumulation is for peaceful purposes; it has nothing to do with atomic bombs, though even they may be a side effect of man's quest for energy. The desire or need for energy is, as we shall see, the cause of all the trouble, a most banal word to use in this context. The problems and subjects which normally affect the people of this country are also banal or Lilliputian in comparison with the Gulliver to be unleashed too quickly and without adequate thought for the consequences, according to the Flowers Report.

Unemployment, the drought, the Government, the Opposition, the TUC, the Olympic Games, Heath versus Thatcher, the Pools – all these are microscopic in comparison with the issues discussed by the Flowers Report; yet the politicians, with their understandable obsessions about votes, will have to decide these issues, and their decisions will be with us thousands of years after they, the politicians, are nameless dust and ashes.

Overheated and exaggerated stuff, this introduction? We shall see, when you have read on and read the report, which needs both time and concentration. One of those two-page summaries and all those private secretaries' annotations and crosses in the margins which so delight ministers will not be enough. And the same goes for the recommendations at the end of the report. So one minister at the least, and his permanent under-secretary, have got a difficult task ahead of them, because the Flowers Report is neither short nor easy to assimilate.

The sub-title of this article (minus the 'not') is due to Sir John Hill, Chairman of our Atomic Energy Authority, when giving evidence to the Select Committee on Science and Technology (Energy Resources Sub-Committee Minutes, 23.1.1974). His statement (paragraph 762) is, of course, the reverse of the truth, because what is under consideration is the accumulation of cancer-producing substances which maintain that capability for many thousands of years, in circumstances where there is no established method for safely disposing of them. (Dreadful as the poison dioxin recently released in Seveso is, the time for which it will persist in poisonous form is trivial in comparison with that relating to such radioactive substances as plutonium.) It is useful to look at some other things Sir John Hill said to the Select Committee's Sub-Committee on January 23, 1974 (numbers relate to paragraphs in the Minutes; observations in brackets are mine).

723. '. . . I think the high temperature reactor and the fast reactor have gained acceptance in many countries'.

'. . . we should now go ahead with the development of our own chosen systems as rapidly as we can'.

728. 'I do not think any limit should be applied to the number of nuclear stations . . .'

744. 'I believe in a large and sustained nuclear programme.'

764. 'I think it would be a perfectly viable policy to say, "Let us decide now to build nothing but SGHWR (Steam Generating Heavy Water Reactor) reactors until the fast reactor comes in". That would be a perfectly credible policy . . .'

782. 'Certainly the Nuclear Inspector said he could give almost immediate approval to an SGHWR, because he has considered the design in detail for the Stake Ness tender of three or four years ago.'

804. 'Yes, I think that is so.' (that the SGHWR is, in fact, a proven reactor). 'There are many fewer technological problems associated with the SGHWR.'

807. 'I think the HTR (High Temperature Reactor) has just about reached the point where it can be introduced . . .'

It is now more than two years since our leading authority on atomic energy made these remarks and no doubt both the canvas and the picture on it have changed since then. The HTR has run into serious difficulties. Perhaps the SGHWR has also run into unexpected difficulties. But the basic problems at the beginning of 1974 were the same as those raised in the Flowers Report and it is surprising, to put it mildly, that the Chairman of our Atomic Energy Authority did not see fit to ventilate them before the Select Committee's Sub-Committee, something which I am sure they would have much appreciated.

The problem can be stated quite briefly: all fission nuclear reactors produce to a greater or lesser extent cancer-producing radioactive substances, which cannot be destroyed, in the waste products resulting from the reactor working in the normal way. The same does not apply to anything like the same extent in the case of a fusion nuclear reactor, but at present we cannot make one of these and we do not know if and when we shall be able to. What, then, should be done with this radioactive waste? Until and unless we can be sure that we are not subjecting future generations to its malignant action, would any sane person say we are right deliberately to produce it? The answer may be a qualified yes, but the scale of production and the existing knowledge of methods of storing the radioactive waste must be taken into consideration before any serious increase in production is sanctioned. Consideration is not a job for a crash operation by that popular entity the 'task force'. Consideration will certainly involve research with its uncertain time horizon.

The present generation of fission nuclear reactors are often described as thermal reactors, in contrast to Fast Breeder Reactors which consume much less atomic fuel, of which we have a prototype at Dounreay in Scotland. Breeder reactors use as their fuel plutonium, probably the most dreaded of all poisonous radioactive elements, because of its toxicity and enormous lifespan, tens of thousands of years.

I now turn to the energy gap, using million tonnes of coal equivalent (mtce), units different from those adopted by Flowers. In 1975 total primary energy supply was 320 mtce including 126 million tonnes of coal of which about 47 million went to consumers other than the electricity supply industry. Based on assessments of probable future growth in demand and the need for electricity, the Department of Energy estimates that the total primary energy demand could grow to about 625 mtce by the year 2000. How is this demand to be satisfied? Oil and natural gas are expected gradually to peter out and become inordinately expensive, and in any case they are essential for the chemical industry. Coal production might be increased, though not to the point where it would provide for such growth. The National Coal Board have projected a production of 150 million tonnes in 1990 and, later, a possible increase to 200 million tonnes. The Department of Energy estimates that on reasonable assumptions about the future availability of fossil fuels, there could be a 'gap' of up to 250 mtce by 2000 and that this could only be met by a nuclear programme. According to the Atomic Energy Authority there would be a need for no less than 33 Fast Breeder Reactors (FBRs) on stream by that time (assuming one-gigawatt stations), apart from a little matter of 71 thermal reactors which would in any case be necessary to provide the initial supply of plutonium for the FBRs.

Essentially the Flowers Report is about whether this number of reactors, particularly the FBRs, is a good idea and, if not, what alternatives there are. One message in the report is to go slow on FBRs and even the proposed prototype Commercial Fast Breeder Reactor (CFRI) which, by analogy with certain other United Kingdom projects, is booked to cost £1 billion and will, I expect cost £2 billion. Another message is, as already mentioned, not to develop reliance for filling the energy gap on thermal reactors until consideration has been given and the research done to determine how to dispose safely of their radioactive waste.

The report deals with what some might term ancillary problems: the sabotage of nuclear power stations, terrorists getting hold of a lump of plutonium the size of a large cricket ball, the safety in transit of radioactive waste and, rather sketchily (probably on purpose) with the alternatives to a plutonium economy. In this last connection, the Department of Energy should have a careful look at duck-coupling, something in which I suspect the Admiralty and the North Sea oil construction specialists may be able to help. Wave power, which is what duck-coupling is about, is supported by the Government to the tune of £500,000 a year. Other energy research, including solar energy, may bring this figure up to £750,000 a year. But peacetime *fission* power R & D is running at £80 million a year or more. Given the doubts in the Flowers Report, is this division of resources sensible?

The following quotations from the Flowers Report emphasize, among other things, the need for two top level advisory organizations, one to do with nuclear waste disposal and the other with national energy policy, separate from and not subservient to Whitehall. The numbers relate to paragraphs in the Flowers Report. The italics and observations in brackets are mine.

282. 'However, the discussions we have had on reactor safety with several authorities have left us with some doubts about whether *the criteria adopted by the NII (Nuclear Installations Inspectorate) in establishing reactor safety are soundly based* and whether their functions are correctly defined.' (May God preserve us! Doubtless we shall be told that there has been a 'communication failure' or that everything 'has been put right' now.)

325. 'The threat to explode such a weapon (a crude plutonium bomb equivalent to 10–100 tonnes of TNT and transportable in a small vehicle) unless certain conditions were met would constitute nuclear blackmail, and would present any Government with an appalling dilemma. *We are by no means convinced that the British government has realised the full implications of this issue.*'

338. 'there should be no commitment to a large programme of nuclear fission power until it has been demonstrated beyond reasonable doubt that a method exists to ensure the safe containment of long-lived, highly radioactive waste for the indefinite future . . . We are clear that such a demonstration will require a substantial programme of research.'

364. 'The impression we have formed is that there is a lack of clarity about where responsibility rests for determining the best strategy for dealing with these (and other) wastes and for specifying the practices that should be followed.'
('These' refers to various radioactive but incombustible materials derived from Magnox and Advanced Gas Cooled Reactors.)

368. 'It is important at such a plant (Windscale where there are about 10 tonnes of plutonium) that the highest standards of general housekeeping (not to do with the 10 tonnes of plutonium) should be employed and *we feel bound to say that we did not gain the impression that this was so at the time of our visit*'. (The visit was in November 1974. Perhaps things are better now.)

391. 'Neither the AEA (Atomic Energy Authority) nor BNFL (British Nuclear Fuels Limited) in their submissions to us gave any indication that they regarded the search for a means

of final disposal of highly active waste as at all pressing . . ., *We think that quite inadequate attention has been given to this matter.*'

406. 'the United Kingdom now appears conspicuously backward among nations with significant nuclear programmes in its consideration and funding of studies related to geological disposal of radioactive waste'.

479. 'we regard the approach to future energy supplies that forms the basis for official strategy as unconvincing.'

510. 'the case for a nuclear programme involving the installation of many FBRs is not yet proven.' (This remark is made in the context of an alternative strategy proposed by the Royal Commission, that the growth in market penetration by electricity should be from 13% in 1975 to 22% in 2025, instead of 60% as proposed in the official strategy. I do not think the Royal Commission gave sufficient consideration to the possibility of electricity generated from other sources.)

511. 'a major commitment to fission power and the plutonium economy should be postponed as long as possible, in the hope that it might be avoided altogether.' ('As long as possible' must mean at least ten years. Is there nothing else in the ten-year pipeline? Serious energy conservation? Coal imports?)

518. 'The strategy that we should prefer to see adopted, purely on environmental grounds, is to delay the development of CFRI. This would provide time for the socio-political aspects of the plutonium economy to be fully investigated and debated, so that the risks could be widely understood and judged before this first step was taken. It would free resources and provide a stimulus for work on alternatives. It would give time for the problems of waste management and disposal to be properly investigated and, we hope, resolved. Each year of delay would increase the prospect of establishing whether a viable alternative strategy existed which would avoid the need for FBRs.'

What about our nuclear power industry and the employment it provides? One could equally ask: What about our ailing shipbuilding industry and the employment it provides? What about our machine tool industry? All pose terrible problems. But it is better to make reactors and the associated boilers and turbo-generators and put them on a desert island – not, in fact, a course I would advocate – than to build and run reactors before we know what we are doing, which is certainly the case in 1976 and will be for a number of years so far as the Fast Breeder is concerned. No British Government since 1939 has had a greater responsibility put on its shoulders than the present one – by the Flowers Report.

Quotations, of which there are many in this article, may be misleading when read out of context. Let us hope they are in this case.

19
THE FUTURE

Address at Imperial College on becoming an
Honorary Fellow and Special Visitor,
23 October 1975

ON behalf of the Honorary Associates and Fellows may I thank you for the great honour you have bestowed on us, an honour for which all of us are deeply grateful.

The most important members of this audience have only recently started their adult lives and may therefore wonder what the future holds in store for them. So, like many others before, I thought I would have a shot at telling you. I start with the difficulty that, though I am pretty confident you will live longer than your fathers and mothers, I don't know how long longer is. But this has the advantage for me of not having to be too precise about dates – perhaps in some cases I shall be out by a mere matter of a thousand years or more.

Trying or pretending to foretell the future has been a human failing since the earliest times. But futurologists have not always been too successful when peering into the crystal ball. In 1925, for example, Bertrand Russell pronounced that 'physical science is thus approaching the stage when it will be complete and therefore uninteresting'. It would be a long job to list the advances in physical science since then. J. B. S. Haldane, one of England's brightest and most eccentric scientists, wrote that he was satisfied from thermodynamic calculations that the energy inside an atom could never be harnessed. Similarly, Rutherford did not believe that atom-splitting would ever be put to practical use (or misuse for that matter). So much for prophecies about nuclear power and the H-bomb which, incidentally, I predict will not intentionally be used in your lifetime, though there will be some troublesome moments. These examples are sufficient to explain why I approach my task with modesty and an appropriate lack of confidence.

Many people, like Malthus in 1798, are worried about the population explosion and, unless the American scientist Calhoun's experiments on the reluctance of rats to reproduce at the expected rate, even when not crowded, have been confirmed and can be extrapolated to human beings, there are good reasons for this worry. If we assume, only of course, for the purposes of illustration, that people will go on having babies at the present rate, by the year 3700 the weight of all human beings on earth will equal the weight of the earth. Some 1700 years later, in the year 5400, if everyone on earth were to be put into a hollow ball, its radius would have to be 20,000 times that of the earth and the ball would have to expand at an alarming rate to keep up with the constantly increasing number of babies.

Some solution of the population explosion is, evidently, necessary; and the need for a solution is one of the reasons why writers about the future and others like the distinguished scientist, J. D. Bernal, predict an exodus from earth to other parts of the universe.

It surprises me that so many writers about the future seem mesmerized by outer space and by Professor Wheeler of the Institute for Advanced Studies at Princeton, in part of whose universe time does not exist, with all sorts of improbable and, in my view, impossible consequences. But nearly all of these writers in spite, probably, of having heard of Crick, Watson, DNA and RNA, fail to realize the equally or more fantastic changes taking place now in the Life Sciences and, with certainty, in the future during your lifetime. Although I shall have something to say about outer space I shall also dilate a little on what you can expect in and from the living world.

One can implant electrodes into a particular part of a rat's brain and, by electrical stimulation, induce the experience of intense pleasure. The rats can be taught to switch the electricity on when they feel like it, and it turns out that the pleasure is so intense that when the rats are presented with their equivalent of caviare or Marilyn Monroe, they ignore these stimuli and continue to press the pleasure button. There seems little doubt – and I think it has been proved experimentally – that the same can be done with human beings. In your lifetime the crude method of electrical stimulation, which in any case would be inapplicable on a large scale, will be replaced by its chemical equivalent, in the form of a pill, Extasin (a descendant of Aldous Huxley's

Soma). I don't know what the chemical will be but I suspect it will be something like catecholamine (familiar to nerve physiologists and some others) but more complicated and therefore difficult to manufacture illicitly.

What may some of the consequences of Extasin be? For reasons of economy and modernity, special issues of Extasin will replace the honours doled out to civil servants and some others on the Queen's birthday and at other times of the year. Some naive people might think that the number of days' pleasure will be proportional to the level of the honour; one day for an M, two for an O, three for a C, four for a K and five for a G. But that will not be the case. We cannot afford to give our most senior and distinguished civil servants four or five days of unmitigated ecstasy because of the awesome problems they have to face each day and which, in their ecstatic condition, they might not take seriously enough. Imagine the Secretary of the Cabinet or the Permanent Head of the Treasury having an overwhelming and, possibly, euphoric sense of satisfaction throughout one week. The concept is untenable – inconceivable – so the quantitative aspects of this new form of honour will require the attention of an Inter-departmental Committee or even, perhaps, a Royal Commission.

Shortly after the introduction of Extasin for this purpose, it will be issued free, to a strictly limited extent, on the Health Service, every Saturday morning.

The Law Court computers may decide, not only for public expenditure reasons, that cancellation of Extasin should replace the present archaic system of prison sentences. If one is used to intense pleasure every weekend, it will be an equally intense punishment not to experience it, quite apart from withdrawal symptoms. Or will the computers come to the opposite conclusion and quintuple the Health Service dose, on the basis that people in a permanent good humour and in a condition of intense pleasure will neither steal, rape nor mug again? Only the computers will tell.

There is also the possibility, though it is not a probability as in the case of Extasin, that intense misery pills, called Miserin, will be developed and replace prison sentences.

I am sure that one or both of these substances will be produced in your lifetime and not only will they be used for the purposes already mentioned, but also in war, or the threat of it. What does a commander do when his troops, pilots, astronauts or sailors become depressed, dejected and apathetic following a surprise dispersal of Miserin originating from a satellite? What might well happen *here* in these circumstances is that gas masks, though in existence, will either be in the wrong place or the rubber will have perished. Some Frenchman, perhaps Talleyrand, said, 'War is much too serious a thing to be left to military men'. In your time war may well have to be left to the anti-chemists. So it will be a race between the dejection and anti-dejection chemists, just as it is today between the SAMs with their changing gadgetry and the electronic counter-measures in the aircraft or ICBMs to be shot down.

The alternative scenario, just as difficult for the generals to cope with, is for all the troops to be in such a good humour that they can't be bothered to deal with the enemy.

So, as is often the case, this particular peek into the future has civil *and* military connotations.

But the next peek does not – it is wholly civil, socially desirable and benevolent. It concerns clones, identical individuals. Within your lifetime it seems certain that we should be able to produce as many completely identical human beings as we wish. The problem for the World Commission on Genetical Control, which will shortly be created for this if not other reasons, is: who does the Commission want? Is it a thousand Harold Wilsons, a thousand Feinbergs or a thousand 1975 analogues of Marilyn Monroe – I leave the precise specification in this last case to your own idiosyncracies? Having reached a decision on these points, we fertilize a human egg with any human sperm in a test tube, remove its nucleus and instead inject into the egg a Harold Wilson, Feinberg or neo-Monroe nucleus extracted from the white blood cells of these characters. This egg will be inserted into a foster mother where it will become an embryo and, after the usual nine months, there will be born an identical twin of Harold Wilson, Feinberg or Monroe. The enucleation of the fertilized eggs and the injection of the special nuclei will be done by Japanese experts (because they are so pre-eminent at micro-manipulation), paid much more, of course, than our Prime Minister.

It is not difficult to realize that these operations will pose rather difficult questions for the Commission. Do we really want a thousand Feinbergs? Personally I would prefer a few Cricks, troublesome as he sometimes is; and you may not wish to have so many Harold Wilsons around, and prefer some Chou en Lai's. Needless to say, the Monroe analogues present different, but, perhaps, more interesting problems. That the operation can be done and, therefore, according to A. C. Clarke, will be done, seems to me a certainty.

I turn now to another aspect of biology in your lifetime; genetic engineering. Of course, you will soon have bacteria 'trained' to produce currently expensive chemicals like insulin and prostaglandin quite cheaply. But there is, potentially, an unpleasant side to genetic engineering and again, I fear, we drift into the military or geopolitical sphere. It seems certain that, again in your lifetime, genes controlling toxins such as those of cholera and *botulinus* will be able to be put into the bacterium *E. coli*, a normal inhabitant of most human intestines. Deliberately or inadvertently, this could cause appalling trouble. A teaspoon full of *botulinus* toxin is enough to kill everyone in London. For comparison, a teaspoon full of cyanide, usually thought of as a very deadly poison, would only kill a busload of people. Although some people think the dangers associated with genetic engineering are exaggerated, I am sure this subject should not and will not merely be left to the good sense of us scientists, even though some nice things to do with nitrogen fixation and food, and with animo-plants, will happen apart from the malevolent possibilities to which I have referred.

Broadly speaking then, you will not have to be satisfied, during your lifetime, with the biological systems that evolution has happened to produce on earth. From now on, others will be possible, by human intervention: that is to say, evolution will be by-passed or short-circuited. Cutting out millions of years of trial and error really makes one think.

I referred earlier to the idea, popular among futurologists and some scientists, that population pressures on earth can or will be alleviated or solved by dispatching people to outer space. You can, I believe, forget about going far enough out into space to have any chance of meeting intelligent beings because the almost inconceivable size of the universe and the velocity of light restrict the probability of such a meeting to the neighbourhood of zero. As I am sure you know, the Special Theory of Relativity does not preclude objects, tachyons for example, travelling faster than light; but then they cannot travel slower. Conversely, things – us and our containers – which travel slower than light, cannot ever travel faster. So the only way to get a reasonable but not excessive distance from earth, say a thousand light years or about 6000 teramiles (the prefix tera means a million million or 10^{12}), the only way would be by deep-freezing the explorers in their spaceship and warming them up just before arrival by a delayed defrost command from within their spaceship (not, of course, from earth). The inmates of the spaceship would, naturally, be re-deep-frozen for the return journey. But there is a difficulty about this idea, which in any case would make no dent in our population problem. The difficulty is that even if one could deep-freeze a human being without killing him or her, the warming-up process would almost certainly turn the subject into an idiot, because our brains do not respond well to freezing and thawing.

This experiment *may* have been done on hamsters. But it is not always easy to tell if a hamster is mentally deficient.

The idea of solving our population problem with the help of outer space, in contradistinction to gratifying man's desire to conquer the unknown, has been developed in considerable detail by the enthusiastic and hopeful Professor G. K. O'Neill of Princeton University, who wants – and expects – rotating cylinders containing you, clouds, lakes, fish, ski-slopes, electric cars, food and other amenities, beyond earth. He even hopes to make the operation pay. Exciting as this concept is, the scientist, as the great Lord Rayleigh said, must get down to some quantitative work to test ideas, hypotheses and observations. The results are rather disheartening. Suppose we want to put a totally trivial number of people, 2000, and their rotating cylinders into outer space. It won't help solve the population explosion, but some may think it the beginning of something bigger, better and more useful. The energy needed to get the cylinders and their 2000 inmates into the best orbit in space is some 15,000 terajoules. It is hard to visualize so large an amount of energy. It is equivalent to half a million tons of TNT and, if one assumes that the rocket propellant is made of the most efficient mixture of hydrogen and oxygen, the cost of the fuel alone for these 2000 man-cylinders will be considerably more than our whole Gross National Product in 1974, a much higher figure than that of Professor O'Neill. But all this is peanuts. Suppose we want to make an equally trivial, but somewhat bigger dent in the world population problem, say five million people into outer space instead of two thousand, though five million is still insignificant, 0.1% of the world's population. Then, the numbers in terms of energy expenditure, money and resources become so outrageous, so incomprehensibly large as to baffle description, imagination or meaning. But have you not forgotten that elixir of life, that philosopher's stone, fusion energy released by the conversion of deuterium to helium? No, even then, in spite of the miracles fusion power will achieve, the answer will be the same – no soap, if only because energy is but part of the effort needed. Goodbye, then, outer space to solve our headaches. Back to the barely heard-of Calhoun? Who will say? Someone had better. That ball filled with human beings that I mentioned earlier is no joke.

Mr Chairman and Rector, your Visitor's cheek is already sore from the relentless pressure of his tongue. The question is – which cheek (it is sometimes rather difficult to distinguish between left and right these days) – he only has one tongue? Whichever it is, his colleagues and he thank you once again for the honour you have bestowed on them today.

20

THE BEST LAID PLANS...

What is planning - what is not planning - what is a planner

The First Israel Sieff Memorial Lecture, 4 May 1976

ISRAEL SIEFF, whom I have the honour to commemorate this evening, had a real zest for life. He not only enjoyed the use of the intellect but also the Bible, good food, good business, good wine, beautiful women and music. He once said:

'The genesis of Political and Economic Planning is found in the determination of a group of men and women to estimate the depth and the speed of the current drift, whither it is leading, and how far it can be controlled.'

These words were spoken nearly forty years ago, at the beginning of the first speech Israel Sieff made about PEP, of which he and others, including one of his oldest friends, Kenneth Lindsay, were proud to be co-founders. He called it the 'Ginger Group of Gradualness'.

Israel Sieff's words could have been spoken today. The 'drift' now is in some respects the same as that which Israel diagnosed. Like him - and I quote again - 'we can see an unplanned and uncoordinated system rocking and tumbling' - around us. But in other respects the drift is different. When Israel spoke, wrote in the newspapers, and broadcast on the BBC, the problems he wanted Britain to face and plan to ameliorate were unemployment and stagnation. Some inflation was proposed as a remedy. Today inflation is the critical problem unless you want what is euphemistically called 'a structural change' throughout the country – remember Lenin's remark about debauching the currency being the best and quickest way to destroy the structure of a nation. And sectoral over-employment, as well as general unemployment, dreadful as the latter is, must be high up on the agenda, though of course, our Union leaders might not agree with this diagnosis. If they don't, must we make ships that will not sail, motorbikes that people don't want or can't get, or aeroplanes that we cannot afford, even if we cannot afford not to afford them? Not at all, they say: re-training will see to all that. We used to make a rather sick joke in the Think Tank, about the Government re-training skilled riveters on the Clyde whose hearing had been impaired by their work, to become bus conductors in Birmingham, Plymouth and London. By the same token Solly Zuckerman used to give a heart-breaking but side-splitting imitation of an imaginary Cabinet meeting just after the cancellation of the TSR 2 fighter-bomber. 'What will happen now to that team of wind-tunnel specialists?', one Minister asks. 'Put them to work on that new thing they call the Pill', another Minister answers, without, needless to say, a moment's hesitation. The sins of the fathers are always visited on future generations. So it will be hard, even if it is possible, to train now, when it should have been done, as a result of planning, forty years ago when the founders of PEP saw the light.

But though, therefore, some of what Israel Sieff expounded does not apply today, none of it is wrong. And the analysis he put forward in the early 1930's is at its most germane to the circumstances of the present day when he says that the real trouble is 'drift'. He pointed to the spectre of drift and told us how to exorcise it, with the support of his brilliant brother-in-law, Simon Marks, at that time Chairman and architect of Marks & Spencer as we know it today. I stand in their shade tonight when I say – and it is almost tautological to say it – that the 'drift' can only be dealt with by conscious, deliberate planning.

When, in the early thirties, Israel Sieff boldly called on Industry to plan, he was taking some risks. Planning then was not exactly a dirty word – worse, perhaps, it was a new and untested concept. Even worse, it smacked of political innovation; it sounded doctrinaire and smelt of the Left. Things have changed. Whether we are Labour, Conservative or Liberal, we are no longer frightened by the notion of planning. We may be bored or irritated by the concept, or even contemptuous of it, but we do not worry about its political implications. Indeed, we take planning, or what we believe, often wrongly, to be planning, for granted. We may not know very much about the subject nor even what it is, but we know that some of it has to be done and is done – somewhere. Rather like sewage; every home should be concerned with it, somehow, somewhere. All political parties have or think they have a number of plans and this has been the case for years. Why then, since we have accepted planning and have done so much of it, or of something masquerading as it, is the country still in what Israel Sieff called 'the current drift'?

Our plans disappoint so often, I think, because we are so supine in the face of their lack of success. At any rate, being a nation of congenital knockers, we almost invariably ignore the cases when things go well, according to plan. When somebody rather jadedly says 'Ah well, the best laid plans* . . .', nobody even bothers to finish the quotation because everybody expects and accepts that plans will 'gang aft a'gley', without bothering to ask or find out why they do, or indeed, whether in fact the best laid ones actually do. Do they in fact 'gang a'gley' because, far from being the best laid, they are not even well laid; or is it because of the people who have to implement them, or because of the much greater number of us who do not properly respond to them? It is important to know, important, I hope, to us as individuals who have more spirit than to live in servitude to what is called Sod's Law, 'Anything that can go wrong will go wrong.' But it is even more important for us as a nation to understand what it is that goes wrong, when it does. For the alternative to an imperfectly planned social democracy, which happens to be in economic circumstances such as ours, will turn out to be not a perfectly unplanned society, but a very thoroughly planned society indeed, under a government which will give most of us negligible satisfaction, much less comfort and none of the freedom to which we are at the moment accustomed. The choice therefore is as follows: either we plan our democratic society well, or after drifting into a breakdown, we shall find ourselves living in a society of the kind so far confined to the other side of the Iron Curtain, or the distal ends of the tentacles as they spread across the globe.

Before considering why plans, planners, or the people who apply plans 'fail', it is as well to understand what a plan consists of and what the process is which is properly described as planning.

* Burns actually said 'schemes'. But almost everyone misquotes the line and says 'plans'.

If we do not begin here, at the beginning, our plans will continue to 'gang aft a'gley' and, indeed, will gang a'gley much after. Let us not begin, then, by thinking in terms of misleading metaphors like 'blueprints' or associated terms like 'programme', since these obliquities provoke emotions or ideas which merely obfuscate or confuse. Nor should we in our minds always be ready to substitute 'plan' for 'policy', a term which denotes something different. A policy, in my experience, usually consists of what is left, if anything is left, of a plan, after the politicians have worked it over. We must – and that is not to use an exhortation with which a speaker tries to belabour a tiring audience back into sensibility but the statement of the imperative which is at the heart of our predicament – we must understand what the process is which takes place when a planner begins his work. Planning is not about this or that kind of society – far truer to say the reverse, that this or that kind of society is about planning. The Oxford Dictionary defines a plan as 'a scheme of action . . . indicating the relation of some intended proceeding'. I like the linkage of the two notions – action and intention. Planning is about the application of rational thought to action for a purpose. My definition is:

> The analysis of systems and situations, present and future, and the construction of logical inferences from that analysis.

The end product of planning is, therefore, a set of recommendations for action which should be logically but not, of course, politically irrefutable.

From this follows the persona of the planner. As well as certain gifts of mind, he must have gifts of character. He must be intellectually honest; all the facts must be surveyed, not a selection congenial to himself or his employer. He must be morally honest. He is going to have to say to himself 'I am not concerned with policy in the political sense. I am only concerned with analysing the situation and with the inferences that follow.' Moreover, he is going to have to say 'I shall eventually come up with a specific recommendation, or a set of specific recommendations, but not with alternatives or compromises for each member of the set.' I mention sets of recommendations since different recommendations may apply to different scenarios, for example to a potential yield of 5000 million tons of oil from the North Sea, as opposed to 2000 million tons.

I hope no-one will imagine, from what I have just said, that I am unaware of the beatification accorded to compromise. Seductive as it is to be on the side of the angels, I see very little role for compromise in planning. You cannot have half a Channel Tunnel. Perhaps we shall find out to our cost in the next five years that you cannot even half devolve.

I may be told that the product of my planning, the recommendation or set of recommendations, is not politically viable. All right, I shall not take offence, but I shall not dilute or bend my end product. A true planner must be a virtuous man. He must not only deploy the dramatic virtues like courage, but the less colourful ones which are more demanding, like tenacity and patience. Planners must be philosophical: they must not mind – get upset or depressed – if politicians do not always embrace their contributions or if they react in other, inappropriate ways. In this connection I once asked a very distinguished Civil Servant what the difference was between Conservative and Labour Cabinet Ministers. He replied 'Conservative Cabinet Ministers grunt, and Labour Cabinet Ministers give us out of date lectures on economics.' My occasional contacts with Cabinet Ministers have not made me feel that this apophthegm was totally false.

Planners must also be capable of very hard work, a phrase not meant to be a headmasterly figure of speech, nor merely a piece of rhetoric. I spoke of planning as being to do with the application of rational thought to a course of action. Rational thought is hard work. It may be that my own resources are not abundant, but I have found rational thought a considerable strain. The great Civil Servant Sir John Anderson once said he did not believe anyone could really concentrate for more than twenty minutes at a time. So much for all those fourteen-hour-a-day thinkers. Interruptions, of course, help them. How often has one heard people say 'I can't get down to my work because of all those telephone calls (or visitors) I get'. But could they have survived without those welcome distractions? Were they in fact capable of concentrating at all? Perhaps those visitors and telephone calls were the perfect alibi for inability.

The definition of planning and the description of a planner

which I have given may go some way to account for what may conveniently be referred to as the failure of planning. A plan put into the hands of a politician is subjected to the test of what is politically viable. Sometimes the results of the test, even by the politician's own standards, are not impressive and consequently the plan may either be dropped altogether or modified. I prefer 'modified' to 'bent', whichever is more apposite. The modifications are usually the result of wondering what people would feel if the products of the plan were applied to them. A new variable, therefore, is at work to militate against what originally was the pure product of reason – the politician's intuition about how people will react politically – a feeling about a feeling. There is, I am afraid, little chance of that pure product of reason preserving its virginity in the face of political intuition, if only because intuition, as Oscar Wilde said, is so often a quick way of coming to the wrong conclusion.

The result is different, but not necessarily better, when the plan is presented to the Civil Servant rather than the politician. Civil Servants are not politicians – some of them would be horrified at the aspersion – but the Civil Servant is rarely a natural planner. Soon after I moved into the room in the Cabinet Office assigned to me as head of the Government's Think Tank, a senior Civil Servant, a man of great ability, visited me and observed that there were as yet no pictures on the walls. 'However', he said, 'it does not matter. If you want your masters to take notice of you, the only picture you will need on your wall is a map of Britain with the marginal seats coloured in red.' The Civil Servant is there to serve politicians. While planners are the servants of politicians in the sense that they are hired and fired by them, and are told what to plan – usually at any rate – they do not serve politicians in the same way as Civil Servants do. The Civil Servant is bound to study situations in terms of what he believes to be politically acceptable and, because he is expected to come up with at least one course of action that will be a political starter, he is bound to produce for his masters a menu or set of alternatives. The planner, on the other hand, should not have on his mind, or in his pen, the possibility that Jack, Marcus, Len or Toby won't like or will contest his recommendation. Such pandering to what is often inevitable will negate the objectivity and independence which are the *raison d'être* for his existence. Objectivity and independence do not, of course, absolve the planner from considering human – but not political – reactions and predilections.

The outer chambers of Ministers are, nowadays, liable to be populated, or even over-populated, with a new breed of denizens, the Special Advisors. These newcomers have not evolved naturally from the local algae on the surface of the political pond; any first year student in political algology can see that they have been imported into its waters from the world outside. When a Conservative Government imports these organisms, it calls them Business Advisors. The Labour Government calls them Political Advisors. However much, or little, Labour and Conservative Advisors resemble each other, they are a very different kettle of fish from the inmates of the Think Tank. I did not know with any certainty the political views of the members of the Central Policy Review Staff. One who professed himself to be a Conservative was more radical than most and clearly more so than another member of the Tank who described himself as a Socialist; and one who claimed to be a Conservative when he came to us said later that he had joined the Labour Party. I mention these matters only to emphasize how unimportant they are in an organization each of whose members should have a social conscience but which, collectively, is dedicated to not 'bending' with the political wind. In the thirties such a declaration of political neutrality would have been said to be reactionary and therefore characteristic of a Conservative. Today, the Establishment having turned itself inside out since then, the declaration must be that of a Socialist.

I must confess, in confidence, of course, to having been tempted to bend on occasions, when I thought the results of a particular piece of analysis would be unpopular, to put it mildly; but when I said this to an influential Civil Servant, he replied 'You are not paid to agree'. So on I plodded, incurring, I felt, some odium in the case in question.

Political and industrial advisors have, perhaps, a different function from that of analysing situations and making logical inferences from the analyses; but if so, they must be clear about this and not confuse the two functions. I am not sure that all of them were or are clear on this point. On the whole, all that seems special to me about these new advisors is that their position combines the functions of lesser politicians with the salaries of higher Civil Servants, and I must admit that that is rather special.

While on the subject of Political, not Policy Advisors, I must say that their useful and legitimate employment raises some questions to which I would like to know the answers. The Government's Central Policy Review Staff, the Think Tank, is a planning organization, within which phrase is included the analysis or dissection of particular subjects – such as Concorde, North Sea Oil and Miners' Pay – and the recommendations that flowed from the analyses. What should be the relationship, if any, between the Tank and the Political Advisors? It is hard to integrate the Political Advisor into an organization which has not got one or other Manifesto emblazoned on its front door. It may then seem sensible at first sight to answer the question of where Political Advisors should be by prescribing where they should not be. But the prescription might be that they shouldn't be anywhere in Whitehall, although I happen to believe that Ministers could do worse than have their own 'Cabinets', as in France. But in that case, some systematization is essential. One cannot just pluck one's friend Professor A from University B, or Mr C from Company D, and hope he will fit in. Nor ought one exclusively to rely on the Civil Service Department's famous 'List of the Great and Good', all of whose members, if I may be allowed to indulge for a moment in my propensity to exaggerate, are aged fifty-three, live in the South East, have the right accent and belong to the Reform Club. Obviously, the selection of the right people for these critical posts should be hived off – a popular phrase a few years ago – from the politicians and the Civil Service; and the independent Selection Panel should not be headed by an emeritus member of either class. But this pipe-dream won't come true. To paraphrase Clemenceau or Talleyrand, no-one seems to be sure which, patronage is too serious a matter to be left to outsiders.

One good reason for pondering deeply on this subject, which really comes down to the question of who should be planning, and who only seems or pretends to be, was foreseen by Israel Sieff when he first put his shoulder to the PEP wheel. PEP, he said, 'gave a creative outlet to many able and original men who, unable to fit, might otherwise have retired . . . PEP gave them an outlet for their energies.' I would not like to try and assess whether there is more or less frustration among thoughtful people than there was when Israel wrote those words; but I feel safe in saying that the frustration he described exists today to a grave if not dangerous degree. Nothing would do more to mitigate that sense of frustration than for those who suffer from it to see that planning, real planning, is accepted as one at least of the courses we are adopting to steer away from 'the current drift'. That is why we need a Think Tank. But is it enough? Should we not also graft on to it a super-PEP or Brookings Institution? If so, it must not be emasculated by that old secrecy syndrome; and it must be located in Whitehall and not, as one idiotic economist once said to me about the Think Tank, at the top of the University Library at Cambridge. (He wanted to be in charge of it, of course). Perhaps I am thinking about a new form of Royal Commission. No-one, for obvious reasons, has a greater respect and admiration for Royal Commissions than I! But I cannot help noticing that their members not infrequently are elderly and retired, or elderly and ought to be retired, or those who have other, whole-time jobs and ought to have the leisure which they so generously forego. The pace is getting a bit too hot for such institutions. A leisurely time-scale, even if desirable, cannot nowadays be made mandatory. There are, of course, a lot of ifs and buts attached to these ideas. Why not ventilate them?

There are other, broader reasons for the failure of minds over matters. Not only are Governments apprehensive about plans – the genuine variety, not the promises and panaceas which gleam like false teeth in party manifestoes; but also, believe it or not, Governments do not have very much experience of them. Governments are prone to get futurology, about which I shall have something to say later, mixed up with their plans for the future. George Brown's much fêted National Plan affords one example. It depended too much on futurology – postulating the occurrence of improbable events – and too little on cold-blooded analysis to have much hope of survival, quite apart from any political or personal problems there may have been.

Political parties are not too disposed to plan in the serious sense when they are in opposition because such planning involves consideration of the future and that implies commitment. Parties in opposition do not want to make real commitments, decisions for the future. They do not necessarily want to know the facts on which decisions for the future may be based, because such facts might well collide with such hoary promises as 'We shall make the private sector more profitable', or 'We shall index all old-age pensions'. To be fair, it must also be said that the party in opposition simply does not have the same access to facts as the Government of the day, even if the facts in question are not secret, or ought not to be. Apart from questions of secrecy, much of the information needed by an Opposition to plan in a meaningful way cannot be distributed to them because the process of distribution would, in the absence of some focal point, take up too much of the time and energy of the officials concerned. I have often wondered why we do not have a Department of the Opposition. I see at least one obstacle, apart from the fact that it might attenuate the fun and games – a description more appropriate than 'cut and thrust' – in which Parliament periodically indulges. The establishment of a Department of the Opposition would imply a loyalty to our country quite independent of any particular political party. This makes me doubtful whether such a Department would ever be created except in so emasculated a form as to make it impotent. Of course, each party would say that the only way to discharge its well-known patriotism would be *via* its own political party, so that what I have just said is nonsense. Is it? I know of several major subjects about which it is, at any rate, alleged that political consensus exists, maniacs apart; and I know of some more about which there certainly could and should be such consensus.

After all that time in Whitehall, I cannot leave it and its departments without mentioning that yet another department is needed – and urgently – a Department of Waste. I am not talking about recycling but waste of the sort we all know about and of which countless examples are available. 'We'd better have fifty copies of that memorandum to be on the safe side.' 'Why bother about the electric light when it uses so much less juice than the electric fire?' It is hard to realize how much we waste in this country and therefore how much could be saved if serious action were taken to minimize waste. To give a somewhat more sophisticated example, the Department of Trade and Industry estimated that in 1971, corrosion cost the country £1365 million. Corrosion chemistry is reasonably well advanced and, where our knowledge is insufficient, the research and development needed would be neither very expensive nor of the 'major breakthrough' variety. That monstrous figure of nearly one and a half billion pounds, five years ago, would be dwarfed if the whole, wicked story of waste was quantified.

You will, I am sure, appreciate, that my proposed creation of two new departments in Whitehall should not add two to the number of departments in Whitehall. The new Department of Waste should see to that.

When a political party becomes the Government of the day, again it is indisposed to plan. There are several reasons for this, but an over-riding consideration is the time scale of office. When a party comes to power, after the crucial period of ritual doctrinaire idiocy when, for example, the Conservatives liquidate the IRC and the Labour Party imposes Advance Corporation Tax – measures both designed, of course, to stimulate British Industry – there is not much time left before one has to start cranking the old machine up, or at least thinking about doing so, for the next election. One must start getting the goodies out of the cupboard and dusting them off. Perhaps the so-called 'best' politicians are always thinking about the next election, a prescription for the mess with which we all are so familiar. Perhaps, God help us, the same political parties should be in office for longer, seven years say, so that there is a reasonable period in the middle when they can forget the shibboleths of the Manifesto, the need to put everyone in a good temper before they vote, and get down to the business of being rational. Something really should be done about this problem of the party's first few months in office, which are without doubt the worst. This prolonged festival, a mixture of the madness of Mardi Gras and Auto da Fé, celebrated by burning anything of a political character which is regarded as inimical, can be a great nuisance, to put it at its mildest. Governments can do dreadful things in their first heady months of office. I wish there could be a law against a new Government doing anything during its first three or so months of existence. Apart from their constituency and parliamentary duties and, of course, their ritual appearances at hospitals, new power stations, Strasbourg and the like, new ministers, even if they have been in office before, should read documents, listen to expert opinion, ask questions and refrain, unless absolutely essential, from taking positive or negative action, activities which, at the beginning of a new term of office, almost invariably create new problems. There should be a period of purging and purification – a kind of political Ramadan.

The time scale is important. Even if a party of coalition Government were guaranteed an ideally full term of office, and this is the most troublesome point, that period would be too short for some essential plans to fructify, which means, of course, that there may be an inadequate inducement for some plans ever to be made. To be worth while, plans must have a practical end product in view, even if it is a long time hence; they should not be an exercise in academic acrobatics.

To revert to the reasons why planners fail, another is that they are sometimes put into bat on a quite unsuitable wicket, though Israel Sieff and his colleagues ensured that this rarely if ever happened in Marks and Spencer. You do not ask a plumber to do an electrician's job, not because he isn't an expert craftsman, but because his skills and tools have not been developed for that particular type of work. Planners, too, have skills and instruments of a specific nature and they must take care that they do not stray, they are not seduced, into incongruous occupations. I shall not, however, describe these skills and instruments this evening, any more than a lecturer on molecular biology has to discuss his spectrophotometer or his computer. There will, therefore, be no discussion of regret matrices, outlook analysis and the like.

Though they must deal with prediction, planners must keep out of the futurology business because *it* is concerned with improbable events, often called breakthroughs. It should, for example, be possible to predict our oil requirements up to the year 2000, if one takes into account the alternative energy sources, coal, natural gas, wind, nuclear (perhaps) and wave power (I hope), which will or should be available during the next quarter of a century. But the predictions, and the plans inferred from them, will be the result of analysing information which is available or which it is reasonable to expect will become available – with a specified if subjective probability – during the time under consideration.

Futurology has its place, I believe, if only to counterbalance the sclerosis of the scientist's imagination, from which I am sure I suffer. Futurology is about what might happen, might being used here not in the sense that anything might happen such as a perpetual motion machine, but in the sense that, given the laws of nature we now know, some things are not inconceivable. Such possibilities require the occurrence of improbable, or even highly improbable, events which are not, of course, certain to happen. The American Rand Corporation used to take a special interest in improbable events and concluded, through a system of consultations known as the Delphi Technique, that the probability of certain specified events occurring increased as time passed, which seems on the face of it reasonable. The feasibility of using drugs to increase intelligence was booked, most probably, for the year 2015. The breeding of intelligent animals for low grade labour comes a little later, in 2025, unless General Motors modifies its assembly line robot and forges ahead with an all purpose one, in anticipation of the Fall of the Auto-industrial age. The Decline, according to my learned daughter,[39] is already upon us.

Futurology, I repeat, has its place; but we must know its place and see that it is kept in it. It has nothing to do with planning for the future because we can and have to do that without postulating improbable discoveries in our scenarios. Let me give an example, again involving our life-line. How much energy are we going to consume between now and the end of the century? What is the optimum combination of fuels to supply the amount of energy needed? We know our coal situation pretty well, even down to its inconvenience cost of 1p/therm in power stations. And we know what miners' pay coal will stand, on the assumption that energy is not a social service. The geologists and seismologists will give us an estimate of the amount of recoverable oil in the North Sea. Warning. 'Recoverable' is a dangerous word without a price tag attached to it, whether one is talking about coal or oil. One would have to know the cost of extracting x% of the oil in the

North Sea before fitting recoverable oil into our energy plan. One dollar off the price of a barrel of oil and down goes that x%; and *vice versa*, of course. The experts' estimate may have a very wide range, say 2000 to 5000 million tons, chicken feed compared with what there is in Saudi Arabia, Iraq, Russia and, I suspect, South America. Let us say there is a 95% chance that the reserves do lie within this range; then the planner can get going. He will need probabilistic estimates of the rate of extraction of these reserves, a rate affected or perturbed by environmentalists and other thoughtful people who think about coal, natural gas, wind, wave power and fusion power. (Rand says around 1986 for fusion power, but I wonder.) Out of all this and more not mentioned, there emerges an energy plan for the country up to the year 2000 or a bit later, because, among other things, that encompasses the life span of our power stations. But if we are ever going to get back into the nuclear power business which, apart from cleaning up mistakes, seems to recede and recede, we must consider what effect, if any, electric cars may have on our energy plan. There are two assumptions in this sentence; first, that people will accept the need to give up exhibiting their virility (or lack of it) in petro-cars; and secondly, that we can make an electric car with reasonable characteristics. The short answer is that we can, but there is quite a way to go at the technological level. And while we are going along that road, some interesting new developments will make their appearance in the petro-car, which is so old-fashioned as to cry out for innovation. Necessity being the mother of invention, the decline of the auto-industrial age may make the innovations come more quickly than expected.

Though, therefore, the planner must deal with future scenarios, he is not a futurologist who, if he is any good like A. C. Clarke, has to steer a course between the Scylla of the impossible and the Charybdis of the just conceivable, for example that some sorts of spoons can be Gellerized or Manningized. The planners of future scenarios are concerned with situations which have a relatively high probability of occurrence within the allotted time, such as that there are not more than 5000 million tons of oil in the North Sea and that quite a lot of it won't be extracted; but that bench mark, together with the other factors I have mentioned, provide the planner with the tools to design an energy plan, or plans, for the country.

All this adds up to the fact that planning involves the future and that while we may, if we wish, love the Rand Corporation and the science fiction writers, we must bridle our affections and not allow them to mess about with our plans. In any case it is the last thing most of them would want to do. We must then be able to say what Israel Sieff said of PEP: 'Through every virtue that PEP could boast, there ran like a thread through crystals, the empirical, the practical, the refusal to get away from facts'.

You may think it odd or undesirably idealistic to be talking about planning when, as Israel Sieff said some forty years ago, there existed, just as there does today, 'an unplanned and unco-ordinated system rocking and tumbling' around us. Today it certainly is rocking. During the last few weeks we have heard Jack Jones tell the Government to hand our oil revenues over to the pensioners. I wish I could have seen the faces of my mandarin friends in the Treasury when they heard this example of what is called 'hypothecation'. Len Murray, the Press said, saved the pound, and then one of his Welsh colleagues immediately wheeled out those corny 'speculators' to explain the tumbling pound, just before our Prime Minister was saying that acceptance of the 3% pay increase, proposed by the Chancellor to our bosses, would make sterling strong again. But why did sterling tumble? Did those wicked foreigners, from whom we have borrowed those Eddingtonian amounts of money, begin to wonder what was going on, who was in charge?

The working week should be limited to thirty-five hours, again according to Jack Jones. Desirable as this new leisure may be, for the pools, the dogs, the horses, bingo and, of course, Her Majesty's Customs and Excise, I suppose you realize that, because of the consequential overtime, this is a new form of company taxation followed by increased prices? Or will overtime be banned? Then he tells us, startling in its originality and novelty, that male pensions should start at sixty instead of sixty-five. Here, at least, I can speak with authority, having been pensioned at sixty by my evil, multi-national employer. I got another job. Perhaps I was lucky; but I did try. Many many people, for whom Jack Jones would be able to speak far better than I, could and also want to try. Should they and I be prevented from trying to get another job by law?

Nobody knows, particularly the person concerned, when senility, euphoria and delusions of grandeur will set in. It may be at forty, or you may be a Churchill, a G. I. Taylor or a David Hilbert, and be fighting fit, intellectually, at seventy. But someone has got to make a judgement and, probably, say what that judgement is: they rarely have the nerve.

So, I repeat, we are 'rocking and tumbling' instead of planning in a cool, calculating and unhysterical way. There is not much time to get back to reality. I happen to believe our Prime Minister and his predecessor understand this.

One of the purposes of this lecture has been to emphasize the need for planners on the one hand and, on the other, for the public to know what planning is or ought to be. The priority is to recognize the difference between the three bent men – metaphorically, of course, not morally – and the unbendable one: on the one hand the permanent and professional Civil Servant with his menu of acceptable and alternative courses of action which enable him to duck the logical inference; the Industrial Advisors whose thinking, with at any rate one exception who is here tonight,* is over-conditioned by commitment to the profit motive, the Political Advisor whose political commitment bends his logical inferences; and, on the other hand, that somewhat lonely and not too popular figure – the unbendable planner.

If we could get our minds clear about such matters we would have a reasonable chance of getting under way the planning our society so urgently needs. There is no logical reason for accepting Sod's Law. It is just not true that everything which can go wrong will go wrong. It tends to be true because we almost invariably interfere with what is obviously right and true, as determined by analysis and reasoning, a process which, so far as I know, is the prerogative of human beings and one which is regularly abused. As I said at the beginning, it is not a choice between planning and not planning which looms for us somewhere in those murky mists: the choice is between a free society that plans well, and an unfree society in which, whether the planning is good or bad, you and I will not be allowed to complain about it. Let us then use

* Sir Derek Rayner.

the liberty we still have to plan the free society the overwhelming majority of us desire.

I end with a few, more hopeful words of Israel Sieff's: 'Beneath the drift we can see the rocks on which we can build a better economic and social life. It is for us to act now, before the foundations are too deeply submerged.'

ANSWERS TO THE QUESTIONS ON PAGE 147
T=True   F=False

1. T.	17. F.	33. T.	49. T.
2. T.	18. T.	34. T.	50. F.
3. F.	19. F.	35. F.	51. F.
4. T.	20. F.	36. T.	52. T.
5. T.	21. T.	37. F.	53. F.
6. F.	22. F.	38. F.	54. T.
7. T.	23. T.	39. T.	55. F.
8. F.	24. F.	40. F.	56. F.
9. T.	25. T.	41. T.	57. F.
10. F.	26. T.	42. F.	58. T.
11. T.	27. F.	43. F.	59. F.
12. F.	28. F.	44. T.	60. F.
13. T.	29. T.	45. T.	61. T.
14. F.	30. T.	46. T.	62. F.
15. T.	31. F.	47. F.	63. F.
16. F.	32. T.	48. T.	64. T.

ACKNOWLEDGEMENTS

I am much obliged to *The Times* for agreeing to the publication of Chapters 2, 14, 17, 18 and 19; to the House of Lords and Miss Mary Furness (Chapter 4); to *Discovery* (Chapter 5); to the Royal Society of Arts (Chapter 8); to the Institute of Fuel (Chapter 15); to the Council, Trinity College, Cambridge for permission to reproduce the address to Sir J. J. Thomson in Chapter 1; to the Librarian of the same College; to Linda Partridge and Benny Fischer (Chapter 15); to the *Economist* and Miss Caroline Atkinson in particular (Chapter 11); to Dr Sydney Brenner FRS, Dr V. Icke, Dr Pat Merton and Prof. I. Talmi (Chapter 20); to Kenneth Harris (Chapter 21); to Cummings (the *Daily Express*), Jak (the *Evening Standard*) and Sir Osbert Lancaster, CBE (the *Daily Express*); to Rothschilds Continuation Ltd. (opposite page 84); to Sir John Hunt, KCB for permission to reproduce the cartoon by Cummings and for advice about Chapter 12; to my mentors Stuart Hampshire and Kenneth Rose for their invaluable and selfless help; and lastly, to my long-suffering private secretaries, Mrs Ann Thomson and Ms Karen Leigh.

REFERENCES

1. SWIFT, Jonathan (1710) *A Meditation upon a Broom-Stick*. E. Curll.
2. ROTHSCHILD, LORD (1951) *The History of Tom Jones, a Changeling*. Cambridge University Press.
3. BRETHERTON, F. P. & ROTHSCHILD, LORD (1961) *Proc. Roy. Soc. B.*, **153,** 490.
4. ROTHSCHILD, LORD (1957) *Discovery*, **18,** 64.
5. —— (1962) *Brit. Med. J.*, **11,** 743
6. WILSON, E. B. (1928) *The Cell in Development and Heredity*. Macmillan Co., New York.
7. AFZELIUS, B. A. (1955) *Z. Zellforsch.*, **42,** 134.
8. ROTHSCHILD, LORD (1956) *Endeavour*, **15,** 79.
9. —— (1971) *J. Roy. Soc. Arts*, **120,** 205.
10. —— (1972) *Nature*, **239,** 373.
11. ZUCKERMAN, Sir Solly (1961) *Report of the Committee on the Management and Control of Research and Development*. HMSO.
12. HARDY, G. H. (1941) *A Course of Pure Mathematics*, Cambridge, p. 130.
13. HIMSWORTH, H. (1970) *The Development and Organization of Scientific Knowledge*, p. 103. Heinemann, London.
14. ROTHSCHILD, LORD (1972) *Nature*, **235,** 296.
15. NABOKOV, V. (1964) *The Defence*. Weidenfeld & Nicolson, London.
16. BELL, E. T. (1937) *Men of Mathematics*. Victor Gollancz Ltd., London.
17. Proverbs, XVI, 26. *Note* The English translation is based on the Talmud.
18. ROTHSCHILD, LORD (1973) *J. Inst. Fuel*, **46,** 25.
19. CAWLEY, C. (1968) *J. Inst. Fuel*, **41,** 315.
20. IGNATIEFF, A. (1969) *J. Inst. Fuel*, **42,** 51.
21. REID, W. T. (1970) *J. Inst. Fuel*, **43,** 43.
22. ALLIBONE, T. E. (1971) *J. Inst. Fuel*, **44,** 85.
23. SAUNDERS, O. (1968) *J. Inst. Fuel*, **41,** 147.
24. WELFORD, A. T. (1958) *Ageing and Human Skills*. Oxford University Press.
25. RUGER, H. A. & STOESSIGER, B. (1927) *Ann. Eugen.*, **2,** 76.
26. BURKE, W. E., TUTTLE, W. W., THOMPSON, C. W., JANNEY, C. D. & WEBER, R. J. (1953) *J. Appl. Physiol.*, **5,** 628.
27. BRODY, H. (1955) *J. Comp. Neurol.*, **102,** 511.
28. DAWKINS, R. (1971) *Nature*, **229,** 118.

29. FRIEND, C. M. & ZUBEK, J. P. (1958) *J. Geront.*, **13,** 407.
30. JONES, H. E. (1959) *Intelligence and Problem Solving* in *Handbook of Ageing and the Individual.* Ed. J. E. Birren, University of Chicago Press.
31. LEHMAN, H. C. (1953) *Age and Achievement.* Princeton University Press.
32. HILL, A. V. (1939) *Notes and Records of the Royal Society*, **2,** 71.
33. ———— (1954–55) *Notes and Records of the Royal Society*, **11,** 14.
34. ———— (1961) *Notes and Records of the Royal Society*, **16,** 151.
35. HALL, G. S. (1922) *Senescence: the Last Half of Life.* Appleton & Co., New York.
36. PIAGET, J. (1970) *Genetic Epistemology.* Columbia University Press, New York.
37. BRYANT, P. E. (1971) *Brit. Med. Bull.*, **27,** 200.
38. YOUNG, J. Z. (1951) *Doubt and Certainty in Science* (The BBC Reith Lectures). Clarendon Press.
39. ROTHSCHILD, E. (1973) *Paradise Lost: The Decline of the Auto-Industrial Age.* Random House, New York.

INDEX

Index

Index